quick & easy

eating for one

IN COLOUR

catherine atkinson

foulsham

LONDON • NEW YORK • TORONTO • SYDNEY

foulsham

The Publishing House, Bennetts Close, Cippenham, Slough,
Berkshire, SL1 5AP, England

Foulsham books can be found in all good bookshops and direct from
www.foulsham.com

ISBN: 978-0-572-03420-7

Printed in Dubai

Contents

Introduction

Cooking for one can be a chore and the last thing you feel like at the end of a busy day, but living alone doesn't have to mean an endless diet of baked beans on toast, ready-meals from packets and trips to the take-away. Cooking for yourself can be a great opportunity to try all sorts of new and exciting dishes and flavours.

With a little forward planning, you can create delicious simple meals from fresh ingredients every day of the week. The recipes in this book are designed for one, so you don't have to divide the quantities as in an ordinary cookbook to make a single portion. They have been created to use a range of ingredients that are easy to buy on a small scale, so you don't have to worry about spending a fortune on unwanted food. If you do want to cook for more than one, simply multiply the quantities to serve larger numbers. Some dishes make two servings, one to serve straight away and one for the following day or for freezing for a later date. Most of the dishes only take between 10 and 20 minutes to prepare and cook and none should take more than three-quarters of an hour. Always gather together all the ingredients for a dish before you start cooking, so that you can be certain you won't run out of anything crucial.

There are mouthwatering meals to suit every occasion from mid-week meals to more special weekend dining. You'll also find a section on snacks and light meals – ideal for lunches or super-quick suppers. There's plenty of advice on making delectable desserts, too, and on stocking up your storecupboard and making the most of your freezer.

Solo eating has never been simpler or more enjoyable!

Eating well

Eating a healthy diet will make you feel great, look good and give you lots of energy; it's also vital for physical and mental well-being and increased resistance to disease. We're all bombarded with advice from nutritionists and government 'experts' and most of us have a good idea of what we should and shouldn't be eating. But if only it was that simple! More and more people live on their own and life is hectic for many of us, with little time for food preparation let alone for making traditional meals, and we often rely on convenience foods and snacks.

The basics of a good diet

A balanced diet is one that supplies the body with protein, energy, fibre and vitamins and minerals in sufficient but not excessive amounts. Achieving this often means juggling what we know we should eat with foods we enjoy and that suit our lifestyle. The key to good nutrition is variety, rather than eating the same meals, week after week. Current guidelines are that most of us should eat more starchy foods, more fruit and vegetables, a little less meat and a lot fewer fatty and sugary foods.

Getting it into proportion

PROTEIN FOODS

Eat 2–4 portions a day.

Protein is needed for both growth and cell repair. Protein foods, like meat, also provide iron to prevent anaemia, zinc for growth and healthy skin and bones, and B vitamins, especially B12.

A portion of protein can be:

- 3 slices (about 100 g/4 oz) of chicken, beef, lamb or pork
- 125 g/4½ oz of white or oily fish
- 2 eggs
- 150 g/5 oz of baked beans
- 65 g/2½ oz of nuts

DAIRY FOODS

Eat 2–3 portions a day.

Dairy foods – including milk, cheese and yoghurt – are a vital source of calcium, important for strong bones and teeth and a healthy nervous system. This mineral is particularly important for women throughout life to prevent the development of osteoporosis. Dairy food also provides protein, vitamin B12 and vitamin A for healthy eyes. To reduce fat intake, try to choose lower-fat versions of dairy foods, such as skimmed or semi-skimmed milk.

A portion of dairy food can be:

- 1 medium glass of milk
- 40 g/1½ oz of cheese such as Cheddar
- 1 individual-sized pot of yoghurt

STARCHY CARBOHYDRATES

Eat at least 6 portions a day.

Around half of the calories in a healthy diet should come from complex carbohydrates and most of this from starchy foods – bread, potatoes and other starchy vegetables, pasta, rice and cereals. These provide lots of energy, some protein and essential vitamins and minerals, especially those from the B group, which are crucial for healthy nerves and digestion. Try to eat as wide a variety as possible, choosing wholegrain and wholemeal types as often as you can.

A portion of starchy food can be:

- 45 ml/3 tbsp of breakfast cereal (or 30 ml/2 tbsp of muesli)
- A slice of bread (or toast or a bread roll/small pitta bread/small naan bread)
- 3 crackers or crispbreads
- 1 medium potato or sweet potato
- 30 ml/2 heaped tbsp of cooked pasta
- 30 ml/2 heaped tbsp of cooked rice

FRUIT AND VEGETABLES

Eat at least 5 portions a day.

Fruit and vegetables provide lots of vitamin C for healing and immunity, and other antioxidant vitamins and minerals. These help prevent harmful free radicals in the body initiating or accelerating diseases such as cancer, heart disease and arthritis, and can also slightly reduce sun damage to skin and the appearance of ageing.

A portion of fruit or vegetables can be:

- 1 medium-sized fruit such as an apple, pear, orange, banana or peach
- 1 small glass (100 ml/3½ fl oz) of fruit juice
- 45 ml/3 tbsp of canned or dried fruit
- 45 ml/3 tbsp of raw or cooked vegetables

■ FATTY FOODS

Eat 1–5 portions a day.

A healthy diet must contain a certain amount of fat to provide essential fatty acids, needed for the brain, nervous system and eyes, and fat-soluble vitamins. However, you should try to avoid too much fat, particularly saturated fat, as this can cause many health problems including overweight and heart disease. Try to eat as few portions as possible and cut down on butter, oils, mayonnaise and dressings, fried food, cakes and biscuits (cookies).

A portion of fatty food can be:

- 5 ml/1 tsp of butter, margarine or cooking oil
- 15 ml/1 tbsp of mayonnaise
- 15 ml/1 tbsp of cream
- 1 packet of crisps (potato chips)

■ SUGARY FOODS

Eat 0–3 portions a day.

It's fine to eat the sugars that occur naturally in food such as fructose in fruit and lactose in milk; it's the 'added' sugars that should be reduced in the diet if possible. There's no need to deny yourself them altogether though, as they add pleasure to eating and enhance other foods.

A portion of sugary food can be:

- 2 biscuits
- A very small slice of cake
- A small bar of chocolate or a small bag of sweets (candy)
- 15 ml/1 tbsp of sugar

Eating to suit your lifestyle

There is no 'right way of eating' and many of us no longer sit down to the traditional three meals a day. However, you should try to make time for some breakfast before you start the day. If you can't face eating, try a fruit smoothie (blend some berries with milk or yoghurt), or at least have a milky coffee and a slice of toast. Lunch is an important break in the middle of the day and prepares you for the afternoon activities. Try to avoid the Danish pastry and bag of crisps (potato chips) temptation and instead go for a wholemeal sandwich and some fresh fruit. No matter what your eating pattern is for the rest of the day, eat at least one balanced meal; you'll find plenty of ideas in the chapters of this book.

Healthy snacks

Eating little and often can be good for you, as it helps to maintain blood sugar levels. However, it's easy to eat too much too often, because of boredom or stress or simply because you didn't eat a 'proper' meal in the first place. While it's fine to eat biscuits (cookies) and confectionary occasionally, don't make them a regular part of your diet. Stock up on healthy snacks and keep a generous supply of fresh fruit to hand.

STORECUPBOARD SNACKS

- Oatcakes and ricecakes, spread very thinly with butter or sunflower margarine if you must, served with a few slices of cheese or a spoonful of good-quality lower-sugar fruit conserve.
- Unsweetened muesli with skimmed or semi-skimmed milk. To add sweetness, sprinkle with some chopped dried fruit such as apricots (these are a great source of iron).
- Unsalted nuts and seeds. These are protein-packed and provide vitamins, minerals and omega-3 and omega-6. Remember though, that they are quite high in fat and calories, so don't eat large quantities of them.
- A small tin of sardines, tuna or salmon. Drain and mix with some reduced-fat soft cheese or 'light' mayonnaise to make a quick and nutritious dip.

FRIDGE FOOD

- Soft fruits such as grapes and berries.
- Low-fat yoghurt (buy plain rather than fruit-flavoured and add your own chopped fresh or dried fruit to flavour and sweeten).
- Cheese, including reduced-fat soft cheeses, which can be spread on toast and crispreads.
- Houmous; home-made or bought (try the reduced-fat varieties, or stir in a little plain yoghurt). Serve with some carrot or celery sticks for dipping.

The well-stocked larder

There's few things worse than returning home to an empty food cupboard and fridge and wondering what on earth you're going to eat. It can be difficult when you're just cooking for one as you don't want to buy in bulk and end up throwing away out-of-date ingredients. However, if you invest in a few basics, you'll always have some standbys to rustle up a delicious dinner in minutes. It will also mean less shopping and you will have the ingredients to inspire your creativity when you feel like improvising.

Sensible shopping

Buy ingredients in sensible amounts and don't be cajoled into buying more than you need – a big bag of (bell) peppers won't be a bargain if you manage to use only a couple. Some items such as dried spices quickly loose their pungency and flavour, so resist the temptation to buy larger packs, even if they seem to be better value. Before you set off to the shops, check available freezer space, so you can take advantage of special offers such as 'buy-one-get-one-free'. You should also check your cupboards to avoid buying duplicates (make an effort to pack shelves logically, with similar foods next to each other, so that you can see at a glance exactly what you've got).

Storage times

Keep an eye on food labels. 'Best before' dates are used on less perishable foods such as dried pasta. The food may not taste quite as good, but it will still be safe to eat a few weeks after the date has gone. 'Use by' dates mean what they say! They are found on fresh foods such as yoghurts and sliced meats. Once the date has passed, you can't be sure that the food is still safe to eat. When the outside of a food such as bread or a conserve goes mouldy, it's tempting to cut off or scrape away the mouldy bit and eat the rest. It's better to throw the whole thing away, as moulds and fungi have invisible toxins that can penetrate the entire food.

Storecupboard essentials

- baked beans and cans of pulses such as red kidney beans
- canned fish such as tuna, sardines and salmon
- canned fruit for quick desserts and canned pineapple, which is useful for cooking

- cans of chopped tomatoes
- cartons of long-life milk
- cornflour (cornstarch) for thickening sauces and casseroles
- couscous
- dried pasta – spaghetti, plus your favourite shaped pasta
- long-grain rice
- oils – olive and sunflower or vegetable
- stock cubes or bouillon powder – if you want to buy only one type, choose vegetable as it can be used in all dishes
- table sauces – ketchup (catsup), soy sauce, mustard and mayonnaise
- wine vinegars – red or white; balsamic condiment

Important perishables

- breads – buy small loaves or freeze half a large one; pittas and soft tortillas usually last a few weeks in the unopened packet and once open you can freeze any unused ones
- onions and garlic – buy small white and red onions and small garlic bulbs
- potatoes – buy a few loose and keep in a cool, dark place to stop them sprouting
- your favourite fresh fruit

Fridge foods

- butter or margarine
- cheeses such as Cheddar and Parmesan
- eggs
- fresh herbs such as parsley and coriander (cilantro)
- Greek-style yoghurt, or crème fraîche or soured (dairy sour) cream – one can be substituted for another in most recipes
- jars of ready-grated ginger and crushed garlic, if used frequently
- spring onions (scallions)
- sun-dried or ordinary tomato purée (paste) – see note on page 71

Freezer foods

- meat, including minced (ground) beef, chicken breasts and sausages (freeze in individual portions) and fish, including individual salmon steaks and white fish fillets
- vegetables such as peas, sweetcorn, mixed vegetables and sliced mushrooms (if you use a lot)

Planning ahead

At the end of a busy day, when you've only yourself to feed, it's an easy option just to open a can of soup or baked beans or settle for a big bowl of cereal, especially if you haven't stocked up at the supermarket. Try to find a few minutes each week to plan the meals you're going to eat over the next seven days. It may sound tedious, but in fact you should soon find it makes your whole eating experience more interesting and enjoyable. Plus it will save your time and energy in the long run, as you won't have to dash out to the corner shop or local take-away because the fridge is bare!

Four-week main-meal planner

WEEK 1

Monday	Spicy chicken and grape salad (see page 50)
Tuesday	Egg-fried rice (see page 112)
Wednesday	Steak and mushroom fajitas (see page 67)
Thursday	Pork koftas (see page 87)
Friday	Marinated hake with stir-fried vegetables (see page 90)
Saturday	Pasta and vegetable ribbons (see page 120)
Sunday	Nut-crusted lamb chops (see page 76)

Check in the storecupboard/fridge for:

Rice, tagliatelle, plain (all-purpose) flour, canned flageolet beans, canned chopped tomatoes, sunflower oil, olive oil, bottled lemon juice, curry paste, Cajun spice mix, mango chutney, mayonnaise, flaked (sliced) almonds, chopped mixed nuts, dried apricots, soy sauce, ginger purée (paste), garlic purée (paste).

Check in the freezer for:

Sweetcorn, peas.

Shopping list:

Dairy: Greek-style yoghurt, Parmesan cheese, eggs.

Meat and fish: 1 cooked skinless, boneless chicken breast, 150 g/5 oz rump steak, 100 g/4 oz minced (ground) pork, 2 lamb chops, 175 g/6 oz piece of hake.

Fruit and vegetables: 1 carrot, 1 courgette (zucchini), 1 red chilli, 1 red onion, 1 large flat mushroom, 1 green (bell) pepper, 1 yellow pepper, celery, spring onions (scallions), 50 g/2 oz broccoli, baby salad leaves, a small packet of stir-fry vegetables, coriander (cilantro), mint, parsley, rosemary, 1 lemon, grapes.

Bread etc: Crusty white or granary bread, soft tortillas.

WEEK 2

Monday	Sausage and mushroom pie (see page 79)
Tuesday	Turkey skewers with couscous salad (see page 58)
Wednesday	Fluffy baked egg (see page 116)
Thursday	Warm bacon and mushroom salad with Parmesan croûtons (see page 80)
Friday	Oriental prawn, pepper and pineapple noodles (see page 98)
Saturday	Shish kebabs (see page 71)
Sunday	Baked stuffed chicken breast (see page 46)

Check in the storecupboard/fridge for:

Couscous, penne pasta, fine Chinese egg noodles, olive oil, sunflower oil, balsamic condiment, red wine vinegar, sun-dried tomato purée (paste), gravy granules, soy sauce, cornflour (cornstarch), soft light brown sugar, ground ginger, a small can of pineapple in juice, garlic purée (paste).

Check in the freezer for:

Prawns.

Shopping list:

Dairy: Butter, eggs (should be plenty left from week 1), Mascarpone cheese, Parmesan cheese (should be plenty left from week 1).

Meat and fish: 175 g/6 oz turkey breast escalope, 1 large boneless, skinless chicken breast, 4 ready-cooked mini sausages or 2 ready-cooked frankfurters, 50 g/2 oz smoked bacon pieces, 1 rasher of lean bacon, 150 g/5 oz lean minced (ground) beef.

Fruit and vegetables: Potatoes, yellow (bell) pepper (should be ½ left from week 1), red pepper (or use leftover green from week 1), 1 red onion, 1 onion, spring onions (scallions), 5 cherry tomatoes, 100 g/4 oz button mushrooms, a small bag of baby spinach leaves, baby leaf salad, cucumber, mint, parsley, tarragon, coriander (cilantro), 1 small orange, 1 lemon (should be ½ left from week 1), 1 lime, 1 small green chilli.

Bread etc: Ciabatta, puff pastry (paste).

WEEK 3

Monday	Pasta puttanesca (see page 124)
Tuesday	Chicken tikka kebabs (see page 53)
Wednesday	Filo-topped vegetable pie (see page 127)
Thursday	Navarin of lamb (see page 75)
Friday	Cod with frizzled chorizo and crushed new potatoes (see page 93)
Saturday	Duck chow mein (see page 61)
Sunday	Guinness-marinated beef (see page 68)

Check in the storecupboard/fridge for:

Penne pasta, fine Chinese egg noodles, sunflower oil, olive oil, soy sauce, capers, black olives, curry paste, hoisin sauce, Dijon mustard, soft brown sugar, cornflour (cornstarch), plain (all-purpose) flour, vegetable stock cubes, dried mixed herbs, bay leaf, canned cannellini beans, canned new potatoes, canned chopped tomatoes, tomato purée (paste), bottled lemon juice, red wine, a can of Guinness or dark ale.

Check in the freezer for:

Frozen mixed vegetables, filo pastry (paste).

Shopping list:

Dairy: A small carton of natural yoghurt, Cheddar cheese.

Meat and fish: 1 large boneless chicken breast, 1 skinless duck breast, 350 g/ 12 oz lamb neck fillet, 1 sirloin or rump steak, 50 g/2 oz chorizo sausage, 200 g/7 oz cod fillet.

Fruit and vegetables: 1 small onion, 1 spring onion (scallion) (should be some left from week 2), 1 carrot, 1 parsnip, 6 ripe plum tomatoes, cucumber, a bag of stir-fry mixed vegetables, 50 g/2 oz baby corn, garlic, parsley, mint, coriander (cilantro).

WEEK 4

Monday   Salmon-stuffed baked potatoes (see page 30)
Tuesday   Spinach and cheese muffin pizzas (see page 115)
Wednesday   Creamy chicken korma (see page 49)
Thursday   Feta and pine nut stuffed pepper (see page 111)
Friday   Lemon-dressed fish with red pepper couscous (see page 105)
Saturday   Spicy pork burgers (see page 83)
Sunday   Peppered steak with potato rosti (see page 64)

Check in the storecupboard/fridge for:

Long-grain rice, couscous, olive oil, sunflower oil, capers, curry paste, garlic purée (paste), a small can of red salmon, ground turmeric, ground coriander, ground cumin, chilli powder, ground cinnamon, cornflour (cornstarch), 1 vegetable stock cube, creamed coconut, bottled lemon juice, mixed peppercorns, creamed horseradish, light brown sugar.

Shopping list:

Dairy: Cream cheese, Mozzarella cheese, Feta cheese, Greek-style yoghurt, butter or margarine.

Meat and fish: 2 chicken thighs, 1 medallion steak, 225 g/8 oz minced (ground) pork, 150 g/5 oz white fish fillet.

Fruit and vegetables: 1 large baking potato, 1 medium potato, 1 yellow (bell) pepper, 1 red pepper, 1 onion, 1 red onion, spring onions (scallions), a small bag of baby spinach leaves, 3 tomatoes, 4 cherry tomatoes, thyme, coriander (cilantro), parsley, chives.

Bread etc: Wholemeal or white muffins.

Making the most of your freezer

The freezer can be an invaluable asset for the busy single person. Individual portions of food are sometimes impossible to buy, and if available are usually more expensive, but the freezer allows you to split multi-packs and to take advantage of 'bargain buys'. When you have time to spare, cook meals in bulk and freeze individual servings to eat later; the recipes in this book have been designed for one, but some make two or more helpings – one to serve straight away and the others to be frozen for a later date.

Ten top tips

- When buying packets of meat and poultry, divide them into single-sized portions and freeze on the day of purchase. Flatten minced (ground) meats such as beef, lamb and turkey to make them easier to stack in the freezer and faster to thaw.

- It's more cost effective to buy 400 g/14 oz/large cans of foods such as chopped tomatoes and pulses. If a recipe calls for 200 g/7 oz, buy a large can and spoon half into a small freezer container to freeze for next time.

- Bread rolls, soft tortillas, pitta breads etc. nearly always come in packets of four or more. Use what you need, then freeze the rest. Some items such as tortillas need interleaving with greaseproof (waxed) paper or baking parchment, so that you can take one out at a time when frozen.

- Many of the recipes in this book suggest using fresh herbs. Once cut, most will keep for only a few days in the fridge. Chop any that you're not able to use straight away and spoon into ice-cube trays. Pour a little water into each, then freeze (you can transfer the cubes to plastic bags once they are solid). To use, defrost a cube or two on kitchen paper (paper towels); the water will be soaked up as it defrosts. This works well for herbs such as parsley and coriander (cilantro), but don't freeze tarragon or basil as they discolour.

- Vegetables with a high water content such as (bell) peppers can be frozen but will be soft when thawed. Although they won't be suitable for cold dishes or salads, they are still great for adding to sauces and casseroles. Slice or dice them before freezing for the best results.

- Freezer books usually recommend 'blanching' vegetables before freezing, but this can be tedious for small quantities. Vegetables that are to be eaten fairly soon do not need to be blanched. Pack them into single portions in freezer bags, label with the date and use within 3 weeks.

- Label and date containers clearly; it's easy to forget what you've frozen and find you've thawed apple purée rather than soup! A 'use by' date is more helpful than the date on which the food was frozen (see below for freezer storage times).
- Thawing must be thorough (especially poultry) to ensure that food is safe to eat – the best place is overnight in the fridge. Do not refreeze food once it has thawed.
- Not all foods are suitable for freezing. Avoid dishes containing hard-boiled eggs, mayonnaise, bananas, salad ingredients such as lettuce and tomatoes, single (light) cream and skimmed milk.
- Keep a supply of standby foods in the freezer, so there's always something to hand when the shops are closed or you've been away for a few days. Mini pizzas, half a loaf of bread (slices can be toasted from frozen) and a carton (not glass – it will shatter) of milk (defrost overnight for breakfast) are all useful standbys. Frozen vegetables such as peas and sweetcorn are also invaluable and, unlike fresh, need no preparation. Add some favourites as well, such as good-quality ice-cream – and don't forget ice for drinks.

Quick guide to freezer storage times

1 month	Unblanched vegetables
2 months	Sausages
3 months	Bread/sandwiches/pastries/cakes Butter/soft cheese Minced (ground) meat, e.g. beef Shellfish Soups and sauces
4 months	Beef/lamb/pork/chicken/turkey Hard cheeses Oily fish Prepared meals
5 months	Double (heavy) cream
6 months	Open-frozen fruit/purées White fish
10 months	Blanched vegetables

Notes on the recipes

- Do not mix metric, imperial and American measures. Follow one set only.
- American terms are given in brackets.
- The ingredients are listed in the order in which they are used in the recipe.
- All spoon measurements are level: 1 tsp=5 ml; 1 tbsp=15 ml.
- Eggs are medium unless otherwise stated. If you use a different size, you may need to adjust the amount of liquid added to obtain the right consistency.
- Always wash, peel, core and seed, if necessary, fresh foods before use. Ensure that all produce is as fresh as possible and in good condition.
- The use of strongly flavoured ingredients such as garlic, chilli and ginger depends on personal taste and quantities can be adjusted accordingly.
- Preparation and cooking times are approximate and are intended as a guide only. The time it takes for food to cook will depend on personal preference and your oven.
- Can and packet sizes are approximate and will depend on the particular brand.
- Vegetarian recipes are marked with a ⓥ symbol. Those who eat fish but not meat will find plenty of additional recipes containing seafood to enjoy. Some vegetarian recipes contain dairy products, so choose a vegetarian version or substitute with a vegetarian alternative if you prefer. Recipes may also use processed foods, and vegetarians should check the specific product labels to be certain of their suitability, especially items such as pastry (paste), breads, Worcestershire sauce and stock cubes.

Sweet treats

A pot of yoghurt or some fresh fruit is a simple and healthy way to end a meal, but sometimes you may feel like something a little more indulgent. Before you rush to the biscuit (cookie) tin, try some of these decadent desserts. These recipes make one serving, unless stated otherwise, but it's easy to make double or more of the single recipes for when you're entertaining.

Cold desserts

FIVE-MINUTE TRIFLE

Put a handful of mini macaroon or ratafia biscuits (cookies) into a glass or individual serving bowl and sprinkle with 30 ml/2 tbsp of sherry, sweet white wine or fruit juice. Top with 75 g/3 oz of fresh raspberries, blueberries or sliced strawberries, then spoon over a 150 ml/5 fl oz carton of ready-made custard. Finish with a spoonful of extra-thick double (heavy) cream or a generous squirt of aerosol cream.

EASY CHOCOLATE YOGHURT FOOL

Blend 15 ml/1 tbsp of cocoa (unsweetened chocolate) powder and 30 ml/ 2 tbsp of icing (confectioner's) sugar with 45 ml/3 tbsp of Greek-style yoghurt, then stir in a further 45 ml/3 tbsp of Greek-style yoghurt for a swirled effect. Spoon some fresh fruit such as raspberries into a tall glass, then top with the chocolate yoghurt. Sprinkle with flaked (sliced) almonds.

FRUIT COMPÔTE

Put 100 g/4 oz/⅔ cup of dried fruit such as apricots, peaches and apple rings in a bowl. Add 5 ml/1 tsp of clear honey, a pinch of ground ginger and 150 ml/ ¼ pint/⅔ cup of apple juice. Cover and leave overnight in the fridge or, if you want to eat it sooner, microwave on High for 3 minutes, leave to stand for a few minutes (perhaps while eating your main course), then serve warm. This is also great for breakfast. Makes two servings.

GRANOLA TOPPING

This is great for sprinkling over puréed fruit or yoghurt or it can be served as a breakfast cereal with milk. It will keep in an airtight container for 2–3 weeks. Gently warm 15 ml/1 tbsp of sunflower oil and 60 ml/4 tbsp of clear honey in a saucepan. Stir in 50 g/2 oz/½ cup of chopped hazelnuts (filberts) or mixed nuts, 150 g/5 oz/1¼ cups of porridge oats and 25 g/1 oz of sunflower seeds. If you like, stir in 15 ml/1 tbsp of desiccated (shredded) coconut or sesame seeds as well. Spread the mixture on a baking tray and bake in a preheated oven at

180°C/350°F/gas 4/fan oven 160°C for 15 minutes. Leave to cool on the tray, then stir to break up the slab into small clusters. Add some raisins, sultanas (golden raisins) or chopped dried fruit, if liked. Makes 5–6 servings.

Hot puddings

PANETTONE BREAD AND BUTTER PUDDING

Make this when you're already using the oven. Take 40 g/1½ oz/3 tbsp of butter and use about a third to generously grease a shallow serving dish. Cut 100 g/ 4 oz of panettone into 5 mm/¼ in slices and spread with the rest of the butter. Cut into fingers and arrange in the dish. Sprinkle the top with 15 ml/1 tbsp of demerara or caster (superfine) sugar and a pinch of freshly grated nutmeg. Whisk together 1 egg and 150 ml/¼ pint/⅔ cup of milk and pour over the pannetone. Leave to soak for 5 minutes, then bake at 160°C/325°F/gas 3/fan oven 145°C for 30 minutes or until lightly set. If you prefer to use the microwave, cook on Medium for 5 minutes or until the custard is just set, then leave to stand for 3 minutes before serving.

HOT CHOCOLATE SPONGE

Sift 15 ml/1 tbsp of cocoa (unsweetened chocolate) powder and 40 g/1½ oz/ scant ½ cup of self-raising flour into a bowl. Add 40 g/1½ oz/scant ¼ cup of soft tub margarine, 40 g/1½ oz/scant ¼ cup of caster (superfine) sugar and 1 beaten egg. Beat everything together for a minute, then transfer to a small buttered baking dish. Bake in a preheated oven at 180°C/350°F/gas 4/fan oven 160°C for 20–25 minutes. If you prefer to use the microwave, cook on High for 2–3 minutes. Serve with bought custard or cream. This makes one generous serving.

BANANAS IN TOFFEE SAUCE

Melt 15 g/½ oz/1 tbsp of butter or 15 ml/1 tbsp of sunflower margarine in a small frying pan with 15 ml/1 tbsp of light brown sugar, a pinch of ground cinnamon and a dash of lemon juice. Simmer for 1 minute, then add a peeled banana, sliced lengthways. Cook for 2–3 minutes until the banana is soft and the sauce thick and sticky. Serve with a scoop of vanilla ice-cream.

snacks & light meals

All the recipes in this book are quick and easy to prepare and cook, but in this chapter you'll find some of the fastest and simplest ones, designed for those days when you've already had a main meal or just want a light lunch or supper dish.

There are plenty of sandwich ideas with flavour and flair – whether you prefer wraps, bagels, pittas or a more traditional filling between two slices of bread. Try hot ones for chilly days, including Crispy Bacon and Cheese Sandwich and the slightly more adventurous Cheese, Tomato and Pesto Toasties. On warmer days you may choose to sit in the garden and enjoy the last of the evening sunshine with a New York Deli Sandwich or Chicken, Rocket and Tomato Bruschetta. But don't stop at sandwiches; the light meals here also include delicious Salmon-stuffed Baked Potatoes with Chives (started in the microwave, so they're ready in just a few minutes) and Halloumi Pitta with Olive Tapenade. And, for those times when you just want to settle in front of the telly with a cup of tea or a glass of wine, bake some Cheese Straws – perfect for munching alone or when friends come to call.

Cheese, tomato
and pesto toasties

Ready in 15 minutes

15 ml/1 tbsp ready-made pesto sauce
4 thick slices of white bread, crusts removed
4 sun-dried tomatoes, drained and roughly chopped
100 g/4 oz Mozzarella cheese, thinly sliced
75 ml/5 tbsp milk
30 ml/2 tbsp plain (all-purpose) flour
30 ml/2 tbsp grated Parmesan cheese
1 small egg, lightly beaten
salt and freshly ground black pepper
30 ml/2 tbsp olive oil for frying

1 Spread the pesto on the slices of bread, leaving a little margin around the edges. Top two of the slices with the sun-dried tomatoes and slices of Mozzarella. Place the other two slices of bread, pesto-side down, on top to make two sandwiches, then press the edges together with your fingers to seal.

2 Pour the milk on to a plate, mix together the flour and Parmesan on another and the beaten egg with a little salt and pepper on a third. Dunk the sandwiches briefly, one by one, in the milk, then dredge in the flour and cheese, then dip in the beaten egg.

3 Heat the oil in a large non-stick frying pan, place the sandwiches carefully in the pan and cook for 3–4 minutes on each side until crisp and golden. Remove with a spatula and drain on kitchen paper (paper towels). Cut each sandwich in half and serve straight away.

Serve with: A sliced avocado and red onion salad

Tips

★ Once opened, a jar of pesto will keep for about 6 weeks in the fridge. Classic green pesto is made with basil, garlic, pine nuts, olive oil and Parmesan cheese. For a really quick meal, cook your favourite pasta, drain, then toss in a couple of tablespoonfuls of pesto.

★ For a non-vegetarian option, stir in some cooked shredded ham or chicken.

Chicken, rocket
and tomato bruschetta

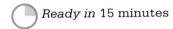 *Ready in* 15 minutes

2 cm/¾ in thick slice cut horizontally from a focaccia loaf
45 ml/3 tbsp tomato pasta sauce
75 g/3 oz cooked chicken breast, shredded
4 sun-dried tomatoes in oil, drained and halved
75 g/3 oz Mozzarella cheese, diced
salt and freshly ground black pepper
a small handful of rocket leaves

1 Preheat the oven to 200°C/400°F/gas 6/fan oven 180°C. Place the focaccia slice on a baking tray and spread evenly with the tomato pasta sauce, almost to the edges.

2 Arrange the shredded chicken and sun-dried tomatoes on top, then scatter with the Mozzarella. Season with a little salt and pepper.

3 Bake for 8–10 minutes or until the bread is crisp and the cheese bubbling. Remove from the oven, scatter with the rocket and serve straight away.

Serve with: A small baked potato, cooked in the microwave until just tender, then crisped in the oven while the bruschetta cooks

Tips

★ If you haven't any tomato pasta sauce, blend 30 ml/2 tbsp of tomato purée with 5 ml/1 tsp of olive oil and a large pinch of dried mixed herbs.

★ There are lots of different types of focaccia to choose from. Look out for rosemary, garlic and sun-dried tomato and olive flavours; they'll all work well in this recipe.

★ It's a good idea to cut the whole focaccia into slices and freeze those you aren't using for this recipe. You can then remove a slice at a time, when needed.

Crispy bacon
and cheese sandwich

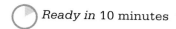 *Ready in* 10 minutes

2 rashers (slices) of lean bacon, trimmed
1 thick slice of ciabatta bread or a ciabatta roll
50 g/2 oz Mozzarella cheese, sliced
25 g/1 oz semi-dried tomatoes
freshly ground black pepper

1 Preheat the grill (broiler) to high and line the grill pan with foil. Trim any fat from the bacon, then put the rashers on one side of the grill rack. Cut the bread or roll in half horizontally, then place, cut-side up, on the other side of the rack.

2 Grill (broil) the pieces of ciabatta for about 45 seconds until lightly browned. Remove the ciabatta (leaving the bacon still cooking under the grill). Top one piece of ciabatta with the Mozzarella slices, taking care to cover it completely.

3 Turn the bacon over and place the cheese-topped ciabatta next to it. Grill until the cheese has melted and the bacon is crisp. Meanwhile, thinly slice the semi-dried tomatoes.

4 Arrange the tomato slices on top of the cheese, then add the bacon slices. Sprinkle with pepper. Top with the second piece of toasted ciabatta and serve straight away.

Serve with: A watercress or mixed green salad

Tips

★ Try substituting turkey rashers for the bacon and cranberry relish or sauce for the tomatoes.

★ For a change, choose a different cheese such as Double Gloucester or Red Leicester. A thinly sliced blue cheese, such as Stilton would also be delicious, but won't melt, so simply grill for a few seconds to warm it through.

★ Ciabattas are available in several different flavours. Sun-dried tomato, garlic and olive varieties all work well in this recipe.

Salmon-stuffed
baked potatoes with chives

Ready in 15 minutes

1 large baking potato, about 225 g/8 oz, scrubbed

olive oil for brushing

sea salt

50 g/2 oz/¼ cup cream cheese

45 ml/3 tbsp crème fraîche or Greek-style yoghurt

10 ml/2 tsp capers, chopped, plus extra to garnish

1 spring onion (scallion), finely chopped

100 g/4 oz/1 very small can of red salmon, flaked, skin and bones removed

10 ml/2 tsp snipped fresh chives

15 g/½ oz/1 tbsp butter or sunflower margarine

freshly ground black pepper

1 Prick the potato skin all over with a fork and wrap the potato in kitchen paper (paper towels). Microwave on High for 4 minutes, then remove the kitchen paper. Brush the skin with oil and sprinkle with salt (carefully – the potato will be hot!). Microwave for a further minute or two until the potato is tender.

2 Meanwhile, mix the cheese and 30 ml/2 tbsp of the crème fraîche or yoghurt in a bowl. Add the capers, spring onion, salmon and half the chives. Carefully mix together, taking care not to break up the salmon too much.

3 Remove the potato from the microwave and halve lengthways. Scoop out the flesh and mash in a bowl with the butter or margarine, the remaining crème fraîche or yoghurt and some pepper. Pile the mixture back into the potato skins. Spoon the salmon mixture on top, garnish with a few chopped capers and the remaining chives and serve straight away.

Serve with: A mixed green salad

Tips

★ If you prefer, brush the potato with the oil and salt and cook in a preheated over at 200°C/400°F/gas 6/fan oven 180°C for 1–1¼ hours.

★ A small can of tuna makes a great alternative to the salmon.

Halloumi pitta
with olive tapenade

Ready in **15 minutes**

25 g/1 oz stoned (pitted) Kalamata olives

5 ml/1 tsp capers, drained

1 sun-dried tomato

2.5 ml/½ tsp anchovy essence (extract)

10 ml/2 tsp lemon juice

1 small garlic clove, peeled and crushed, or 2.5 ml/½ tsp garlic purée (paste)

freshly ground black pepper

100 g/4 oz Halloumi cheese, drained and sliced

2 mini pitta breads, warmed

rocket leaves, red onion slices and wedges of lemon to garnish

1 To make the olive tapenade, finely chop the olives, capers and sun-dried tomato. Put them in a bowl with the anchovy essence, lemon juice, garlic and a little pepper. Stir everything together and set aside.

2 Heat a non-stick griddle pan or frying pan until hot, then turn down the heat. Add the Halloumi and cook for 4–5 minutes, turning half-way through the cooking time. Remove and set aside.

3 Warm the pitta breads for about 20 seconds on each side, then open them up and fill them with the Halloumi and the olive tapenade. Garnish with rocket, onion slices and wedges of lemon. Serve straight away while the Halloumi is still warm.

Serve with: A lightly dressed green salad

Tips

★ Make double this quantity of the tapenade and save half in a covered dish in the fridge. It will keep for 3–4 days. It's delicious as a snack spread on unsalted crackers or toasted ciabatta.

★ Don't add any salt when seasoning the tapenade; there's already plenty in the olives, anchovy essence and cheese.

★ For vegetarians, leave out the anchovy essence and add a dash of soy sauce instead.

Pepperoni and Mozzarella
onion bagel

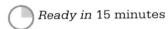 *Ready in* 15 minutes

10 ml/2 tsp olive oil

1 small onion, peeled and thinly sliced

1 large onion bagel

45 ml/3 tbsp pizza sauce topping

25 g/1 oz sliced pepperoni

50 g/2 oz/½ cup grated Mozzarella cheese

basil leaves to garnish (optional)

1 Heat the oil in a small non-stick frying pan, add the onion and cook gently for 10 minutes or until soft, stirring frequently.

2 Preheat the grill (broiler) to hot and line the grill pan with foil. Carefully cut the bagel horizontally into three slices and spread each slice with 15 ml/ 1 tbsp of the pizza topping. Arrange the onion and pepperoni on top. Sprinkle with the Mozzarella.

3 Place the bagel slices on the grill rack and cook for about 5 minutes or until the cheese has melted and is bubbling and the pepperoni is sizzling. Serve straight away, scattered with basil leaves, if liked.

Serve with: A cherry tomato and cucumber salad or some ready-made coleslaw

Tips

★ If you prefer, cut the bagel in half instead of into three slices and be more generous with the topping on each.

★ There are many different flavoured savoury bagels that could be used for this recipe; wholemeal, caraway seed and sesame seed varieties would all work well.

★ If you haven't any pizza topping sauce, blend 30 ml/2 tbsp of sun-dried tomato purée (paste) with 10 ml/2 tsp of olive oil and 2.5 ml/½ tsp of dried mixed herbs.

New York
deli sandwich

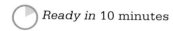 *Ready in* 10 minutes

3 slices of white, wholemeal or granary bread
softened butter or sunflower margarine for spreading
1 thick slice of corned beef
10 ml/2 tsp American made mustard
½ red onion, peeled and sliced
a handful of salad leaves
2 whole pickled chillies to garnish

1 Thinly spread the bread with butter or margarine. Put the corned beef on one slice of the bread, spread with the mustard, then scatter with the onion slices.

2 Top with the second slice of bread. Put the salad leaves on top, then add the final slice of bread, buttered-side down.

3 Cut the sandwich in half diagonally and garnish each half with a whole pickled chilli, held in place with a cocktail stick (toothpick).

Serve with: Cornichons and some plain salted crisps (potato chips)

Tips

★ Use thinly sliced bread to make these sandwiches, or they'll be too big to handle and eat.

★ Alternative sandwich suggestions:

– canned tuna, capers and sweetcorn, blended with lemon mayonnaise

– low-fat soft cheese, peanut butter and grated carrot

– mashed canned sardines and finely sliced fennel

– smoked salmon or trout sprinkled with lime juice and freshly ground black pepper and avocado slices

★ If you need to make the sandwich ahead, wrap it tightly in clingfilm (plastic wrap) and keep it chilled in the fridge for no more than 4 hours.

Sandwich steak
and guacamole wrap

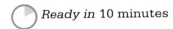 *Ready in* 10 minutes

5 ml/1 tsp olive oil
1 beef 'sandwich' steak, about 50 g/2 oz
salt and freshly ground black pepper
1 soft flour tortilla
60 ml/4 tbsp bought guacamole
a handful of frisée or baby lettuce leaves
½ small red onion, peeled and thinly sliced

1 Heat the oil in a non-stick frying or griddle pan. Add the steak and fry over a medium heat for 1–1½ minutes on each side, depending on how well you like it cooked. Remove it from the pan, and place it on a board. Lightly season with salt and pepper and leave it to 'rest' for a couple of minutes.

2 Quickly wipe the pan clean with kitchen paper (paper towels). Add the tortilla to the pan and warm it for about 30 seconds on each side.

3 Place the tortilla on a plate and spread thickly with the guacamole. Scatter the lettuce leaves and onion slices down the centre of the tortilla. Thinly slice the beef into strips and place on top of the salad ingredients. Roll up and eat straight away.

Serve with: Tortilla chips and a fresh tomato salsa or a chopped
beefsteak tomato

Tips

★ If you don't like raw onions, fry the slices gently in a little oil before cooking the steak.

★ 'Sandwich' steak, also known as 'minute' steak, is thinly sliced beef that has been gently beaten with a meat mallet to tenderise it. It is slightly cheaper than rump or fillet steak, but you could use one of these if you prefer.

★ To make your own guacamole, peel and roughly dice 1 small ripe avocado and mash the flesh with 15 ml/1 tbsp of fresh or bottled lime juice, 15 ml/1 tbsp of Greek-style yoghurt, a dash of Tabasco sauce and salt and pepper to taste.

Cheese straws

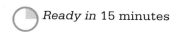 *Ready in* 15 minutes

375 g/13 oz packet of ready-rolled puff pastry (paste)
50 g/2 oz mature Cheddar cheese, finely grated
25 g/1 oz Parmesan cheese, finely grated
1.5 ml/¼ tsp cayenne pepper
freshly ground black pepper
30 ml/2 tbsp milk

1 Remove the pastry from the fridge and leave, still in its packet, at room temperature for 5 minutes (this makes it less likely to crack when unrolling). Preheat the oven to 190°C/375°F/gas 5/fan oven 170°C and line two baking (cookie) sheets with non-stick baking parchment.

2 Mix the cheeses with the cayenne and a good sprinkling of black pepper.

3 Carefully unroll the pastry on a board or a lightly floured clean work surface. Brush the pastry all over with the milk, then sprinkle with the grated cheese mixture. Cut into 1 cm/½ in x 10 cm/4 in strips and place on the baking sheets, spacing them slightly apart to allow room for rising.

4 Bake for 10–12 minutes or until the strips are well risen, golden-brown and crisp. Leave to cool on the baking sheets for 1 minute, then transfer to a wire rack.

Makes about 60

Tips

★ These are delicious served hot or, if you prefer, cool them completely, then store in an airtight container for up to 2 days. They can be rewarmed in a preheated hot oven for a few minutes.

★ For a change, make Cheese and Walnut Palmiers: unroll the pastry and cut it lengthways into four long strips. Brush each strip all over with lightly beaten egg, then sprinkle with a mixture of 75 g/3 oz/¾ cup of very finely chopped walnut pieces and 50 g/2 oz/½ cup of finely grated Cheddar. Run a rolling pin gently over the mixture to press it into the pastry. Roll up the strips, one at a time, from one short edge to the centre, then roll up the other side until the two rolls meet. Brush the part where the rolls meet with a little beaten egg. Using a sharp knife, cut the pastry into 1 cm/½ in slices. Repeat with the remaining pastry strips. Transfer the slices to baking sheets lined with non-stick baking parchment and bake for 12–15 minutes or until well risen and golden-brown.

chicken turkey & duck

For succulence, flavour and versatility, chicken is hard to beat. Because it's naturally tender, it's ideal for quick cooking and there are many cuts to choose from to suit solo servings. As well as the familiar breasts, quarters, thighs and drumsticks, you'll also find goujons – thin strips of breast meat – which are brilliant for stir-fries and curries; and escalopes – skinned and flattened chicken breasts – that can be tossed in seasoned flour and pan-fried in less than 5 minutes.

Lean and healthy, chicken is full of protein and B vitamins and, if you're trying to reduce your red meat intake, minced chicken makes an excellent alternative to minced beef, lamb or pork in most dishes.

Generally, chicken portions are less expensive if bought in larger packs, so straight after purchase, split them into individual servings, wrap them well and freeze any that you won't be using within a day or two. They will keep for up to 3 months in the freezer; defrost overnight in the fridge and always check that the chicken is thoroughly thawed before cooking. You should also make sure that it is thoroughly cooked before serving by piercing the flesh at the thickest point; the juices should run clear and not be at all pink.

Chicken
and vegetable noodles

Ready in 15 minutes

50 g/2 oz dried flat rice noodles

10 ml/2 tsp finely shredded fresh root ginger or ginger paste from a jar

15 ml/1 tbsp mirin, dry rice wine or sherry

10 ml/2 tsp soy sauce

1 skinless, boneless chicken breast, cut into thin strips

10 ml/2 tsp sunflower oil

100 g/4 oz Chinese mixed stir-fry vegetables

75 ml/5 tbsp chicken or vegetable stock

10 ml/2 tsp oyster sauce (optional)

freshly ground black pepper

1 Place the noodles in a bowl and pour over plenty of boiling water to cover. Soak for 3–4 minutes, then drain and rinse gently under cold running water to cool (this stops the noodles from cooking further). Drain again and set aside.

2 Combine the ginger, mirin, rice wine or sherry and soy sauce in a bowl, then add the chicken strips. Stir everything together to coat the chicken.

3 Heat the oil in a frying pan, preferably non-stick. Remove the chicken from the marinade, add to the pan and cook over a high heat for 1–2 minutes, stirring all the time, until lightly browned. Add the vegetables and cook for a further 1 minute, then pour in the stock and marinade.

4 Bring to the boil, then stir and cook over a high heat for 2–3 minutes. Add the oyster sauce, if using, and noodles. Stir to mix well and cook for 1–2 minutes or until the chicken, vegetables and noodles are cooked and tender. Remove from the heat, season with pepper and serve immediately.

Tips

* Strips of turkey escalope, pork fillet or lean rump steak would make an excellent alternative to chicken in this recipe.

* Instead of buying a bag of Chinese stir-fry vegetables, you could use your favourite stir-fry vegetables, such as mangetout (snow peas), baby sweetcorn, carrots, red (bell) peppers and mushrooms, all cut into even-sized pieces.

* If you haven't any mirin, rice wine or sherry, use orange juice instead.

Baked stuffed chicken breast

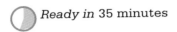 *Ready in* 35 minutes

1 large skinless, boneless chicken breast

10 ml/2 tsp fresh or bottled lemon juice

15 ml/1 tbsp finely chopped fresh herbs such as tarragon and parsley

1 small garlic clove, peeled and crushed, or 2.5 ml/½ tsp garlic purée (paste)

salt and freshly ground black pepper

1 rasher (slice) of lean bacon

1 Preheat the oven to 200°C/400°F/gas 6/fan oven 180°C. Put the chicken breast on a board and, using a small, sharp knife, make a slit in the side to create a little pocket.

2 Mix together the lemon juice, herbs, garlic and a little salt and pepper. Push the mixture into the chicken pocket. Wrap the chicken in the bacon rasher and secure in place with a wooden cocktail stick (toothpick).

3 Place the chicken on a baking (cookie) sheet lined with baking parchment. Bake for 20–25 minutes or until the chicken is cooked through. Remove from the oven and allow to rest for a couple of minutes before cutting into thick slices and serving.

Serve with: Steamed asparagus and wedges of lemon and tomato

Tip

★ A jacket potato would make a great accompaniment to the chicken. Scrub a large potato, weighing about 225 g/8 oz, and prick the skin several times with a fork. Microwave it on High for 3 minutes, then rub the skin with a little oil and salt, if liked (carefully – the potato will be hot!). Finish it in the oven, either on a baking tray or directly on the oven shelf, when adding the chicken.

Creamy chicken korma

Ready in 40 minutes

15 ml/1 tbsp sunflower oil

2 skinned chicken thighs, on the bone

½ small onion, peeled and finely chopped

1 garlic clove, crushed, or 5 ml/1 tsp garlic purée (paste)

1.5 ml/¼ tsp ground turmeric

5 ml/1 tsp ground coriander

2.5 ml/½ tsp ground cumin

a pinch of chilli powder

a pinch of ground cinnamon

2.5 ml/½ tsp cornflour (cornstarch)

30 ml/2 tbsp plain or Greek-style yoghurt

50 ml/2 fl oz chicken or vegetable stock

15 g/½ oz creamed coconut, chopped

salt and freshly ground black pepper

15 ml/1 tbsp chopped fresh coriander (cilantro)

1 red chilli, sliced, to garnish (optional)

1 Heat the oil in a small non-stick frying pan, add the chicken thighs and cook for 3–4 minutes or until lightly browned. Remove with a slotted spoon, leaving any oil and juices behind, and set aside.

2 Add the onion to the pan and cook gently for 5 minutes until almost tender. Turn down the heat to very low, then stir in the garlic, followed by the dry spices. Cook for a few more seconds.

3 Blend the cornflour with the yoghurt and stir into the spicy mixture. Gradually add the stock, then stir in the creamed coconut and a little salt and pepper.

4 Return the chicken to the pan, half-cover with a lid and cook gently for a further 10 minutes or until the chicken is cooked through. Serve straight away, scattered with the chopped coriander and chilli slices, if using.

Serve with: Steamed or boiled rice, naan breads or popadoms

Tip

★ Don't let the long list of ingredients for this recipe put you off; it's still really quick and simple. If you prefer, use 10 ml/2 tsp of bought mild curry powder or korma paste instead of the combination of dry spices.

Spicy chicken
and grape salad

Ready in 15 minutes

10 ml/2 tsp curry paste

15 ml/1 tbsp mango chutney

15 ml/1 tbsp mayonnaise

30 ml/2 tbsp Greek-style yoghurt

5 ml/1 tsp fresh or bottled lemon juice

salt and freshly ground black pepper

1 cooked skinless, boneless chicken breast, cut into bite-sized pieces

15 ml/1 tbsp toasted flaked (slivered) almonds

50 g/2 oz red and green seedless grapes, halved

25 g/1 oz ready-to-eat dried apricots, chopped

¼ green (bell) pepper, seeded and sliced

1 celery stick, sliced

2 spring onions (scallions), trimmed and sliced

2 handfuls of baby salad leaves

1   Blend together the curry paste, chutney, mayonnaise, yoghurt, lemon juice and a little salt and pepper in a mixing bowl. Add the chicken to the sauce and stir to coat.

2   Mix together the almonds, grapes, apricots, sliced pepper, celery and spring onions. Reserve a quarter for the garnish, then stir the rest into the chicken mixture.

3   Serve the spicy chicken salad on a bed of baby salad leaves and scatter the reserved garnish over the top before serving.

Serve with: Crusty white or granary bread

Tip

★   Make double the quantity of spicy chicken and store half in an airtight container in the fridge. Serve the following day as a jacket potato topping or as a chunky filling for pitta bread or a flour tortilla wrap.

Chicken tikka
kebabs

 Ready in 20 minutes

1 large skinless, boneless chicken breast
75 ml/5 tbsp natural yoghurt
15 ml/1 tbsp chopped fresh mint
10 ml/2 tsp tandoori curry paste
5 cm/2 in piece of cucumber, coarsely grated
1 small garlic clove, peeled and crushed, or 2.5 ml/½ tsp garlic purée (paste)
salt and freshly ground black pepper
wedges of lime
chopped fresh coriander (cilantro) to garnish (optional)

1 Cut the chicken breast into six chunks. Mix together half the yoghurt, 5 ml/1 tsp of the mint and the curry paste. Stir in the chicken. Set aside for a few minutes while making the cucumber dip.

2 Squeeze out some of the juices from the cucumber. Put the cucumber in a bowl with the remaining yoghurt and mint and the garlic. Season well, then stir together and chill until ready to serve.

3 Preheat the grill (broiler) to high and line the grill pan with foil. Thread the chicken pieces on to two skewers and place on the grill rack. Grill (broil) for 10–12 minutes, turning a few times, until the chicken is cooked through.

4 Serve the chicken tikka kebabs with the cucumber dip and wedges of lime. Garnish with chopped coriander, if liked.

Serve with: Mixed-grain rice

Tips

★ Let the chicken chunks marinate for 30 minutes before cooking, if you have time. This not only allows the flavour to penetrate the meat but also helps to tenderise it.

★ Use a turkey breast escalope, about 175 g/6 oz, instead of the chicken breast, if you prefer.

★ Mixed-grain rice takes about 20 minutes, so start cooking it before you prepare the kebabs. For a simple alternative, serve the chicken kebabs with naan breads, warmed under the grill for about 1 minute.

Linguine with chicken
and asparagus

Ready in 10 minutes

100 g/4 oz dried linguine

30 ml/2 tbsp olive oil

100 g/4 oz chicken breast fillets, trimmed and cut into thin strips

75 g/3 oz fine asparagus, trimmed

5 ml/1 tsp grated lemon zest

juice of ½ lemon

salt and freshly ground black pepper

snipped chives and slices of lemon to garnish (optional)

1 Cook the pasta in plenty of boiling lightly salted water for 8–10 minutes, or according to the packet instructions, until *al dente* (tender but still firm to the bite).

2 Meanwhile, heat the oil in a non-stick frying pan, add the chicken and stir-fry for 2 minutes until beginning to colour. Add the asparagus, lemon zest and juice and cook for a further 3 minutes. Season to taste with a little salt and pepper.

3 Drain the pasta and pile on to a warmed plate. Add the chicken strips and asparagus, then garnish with chives and slices of lemon, if liked. Serve straight away.

Tips

★ You should be able to work out the weight of pasta you need from the packet size. If not, a mug is quicker and easier than using weighing scales. A mugful of small pasta shapes weighs about 100 g/4 oz; a mugful of large pasta shapes about 50 g/2 oz.

★ Lime zest and juice make a great alternative to lemon; use a dash more lime juice, though, as it is less acidic and has a sweeter flavour.

★ If liked, toss the pasta in a tablespoonful or two of crème fraîche or soured (dairy sour) cream for a richer flavour.

Italian-style
balsamic chicken

Ready in 15 minutes

1 skinless, boneless chicken breast
15 g/½ oz/1 tbsp butter, softened
1 small garlic clove, crushed, or 2.5 ml/½ tsp garlic purée (paste)
5 ml/1 tsp clear honey
10 ml/2 tsp balsamic condiment
salt and freshly ground black pepper
a few fresh basil leaves to garnish

1 Trim the chicken breast, if necessary, then place between two sheets of clingfilm (plastic wrap) or baking parchment. Gently beat with a meat mallet or rolling pin to an even thickness.

2 Preheat the grill (broiler) to medium-hot and line the grill pan with foil. Mix together the remaining ingredients, seasoning with a little salt and pepper, and spread over both sides of the chicken. Place the chicken on the grill (broiler) rack and cook for 4–5 minutes.

3 Turn the chicken over, baste with the pan juices and grill (broil) for a further 5 minutes or until cooked through. Serve straight away, garnished with basil leaves, with any remaining pan juices drizzled over.

Serve with: Grilled cherry vine tomatoes, wedges of lemon, and linguine or tagliatelle pasta

Tips

★ You can buy jars of garlic paste (purée) in the supermarket. It's especially good for those recipes when you want only a tiny amount of garlic and once opened will keep in the fridge for a couple of months.

★ Balsamic condiment is rich, dark and mellow. Made in Modena in Northern Italy, it is fermented from grape juice for a minimum of 4 years and the most expensive versions for up to 40 years. It has a unique flavour, so don't use ordinary vinegar as a substitute in this dish.

Turkey skewers
with couscous salad

 Ready in 25 minutes

50 g/2 oz/⅓ cup couscous
75 ml/3 fl oz boiling water or stock
1 turkey breast escalope, about 175 g/6 oz
½ yellow (bell) pepper, seeded and cut into chunks
1 small red onion, peeled and cut into wedges
15 ml/1 tbsp olive oil
juice and zest of ½ small lemon
15 ml/1 tbsp chopped fresh tarragon
salt and freshly ground black pepper
1 small orange, peeled and chopped
5 cm/2 in piece of cucumber, diced
15 ml/1 tbsp chopped fresh mint

1 Put the couscous in a bowl and pour the boiling water or stock over. Stir, then set aside to cool and to allow the liquid to be absorbed.

2 Cut the turkey into bite-sized pieces and put in a bowl with the pepper chunks and onion. Drizzle with the oil and lemon juice, then scatter the lemon zest, tarragon and a little salt and pepper over. Toss together to mix well.

3 Preheat the grill (broiler) to high and line the grill pan with foil. Thread the turkey, pepper and onion on to two metal or bamboo skewers and place on the grill pan. Grill (broil) for 10–12 minutes, turning a few times, until the turkey and vegetables are cooked through.

4 Fluff up the couscous with a fork and stir through the orange, cucumber and mint. Serve the turkey skewers on the couscous.

Tips

★ If you're using bamboo skewers under the grill or on a barbecue, soaking them in cold water for a few minutes before using helps to stop them burning.

★ Make double this quantity of the couscous salad and serve half the following day with grilled fish or cold sliced meats.

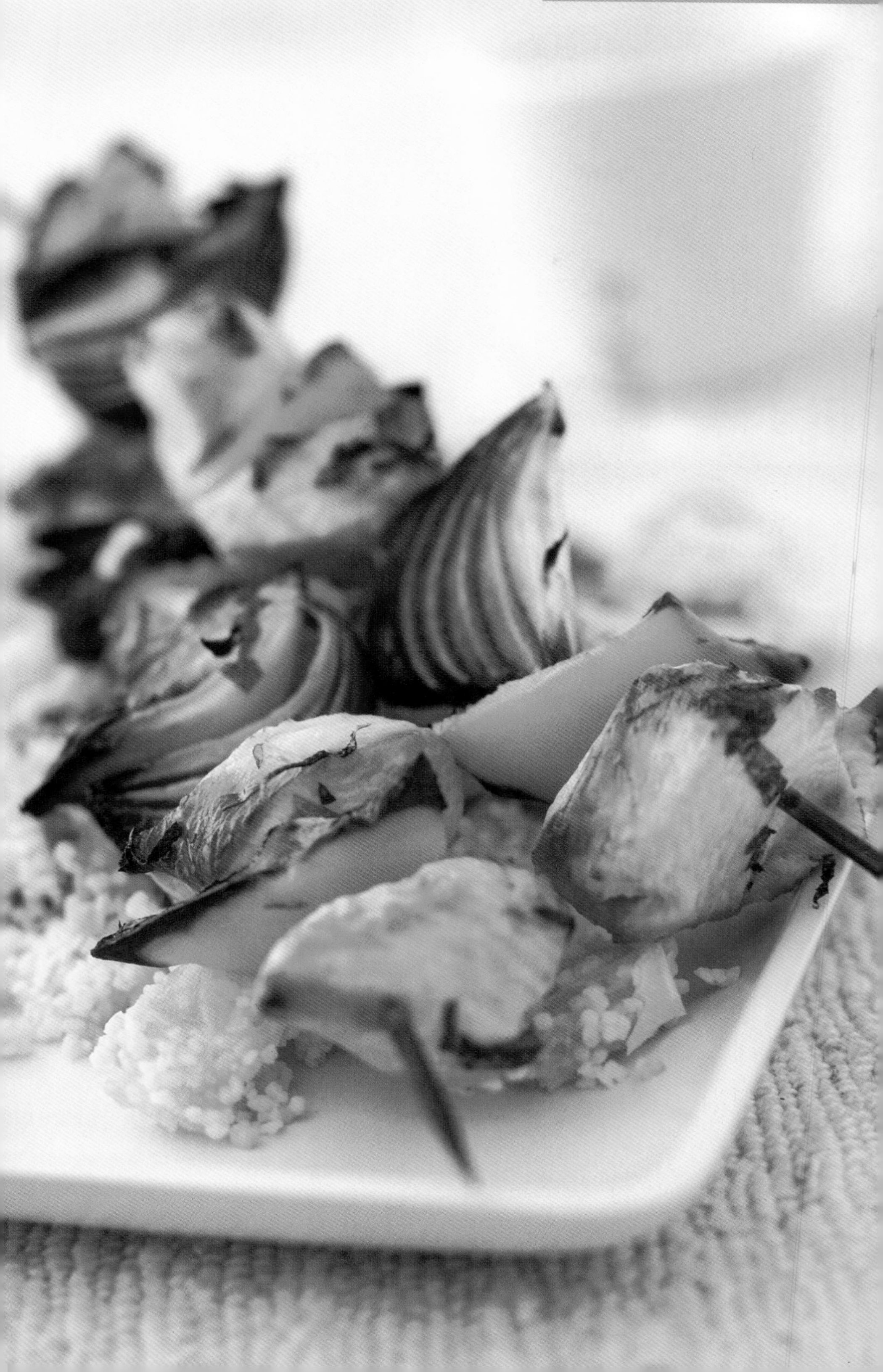

Duck and vegetable
chow mein

 Ready in 15 minutes

50 g/2 oz fine egg noodles

15 ml/1 tbsp sunflower oil

1 skinless duck breast, cut into strips

1 small garlic clove, crushed, or 2.5 ml/½ tsp garlic purée (paste)

1 spring onion (scallion), sliced

100 g/4 oz stir-fry mixed vegetables such as carrots, Chinese leaf, broccoli, red (bell) pepper and beansprouts

50 g/2 oz baby corn

10 ml/2 tsp hoisin sauce

50 ml/2 fl oz hot chicken or vegetable stock

2.5 ml/½ tsp cornflour (cornstarch)

10 ml/2 tsp cold water

1 Cook the noodles in boiling lightly salted water for 3 minutes or according to the packet instructions. Drain well and set aside.

2 Meanwhile, heat half the oil in a non-stick frying pan, add the duck and stir-fry for 3–4 minutes. Remove from the pan with a slotted spoon, leaving the fat and juices behind. Set aside on a plate.

3 Add the remaining oil to the pan. Add the garlic, spring onion, vegetables and corn and stir-fry for 1 minute. Return the duck to the pan and add the hoisin sauce and stock.

4 Blend together the cornflour and water, then stir into the pan. Cook for 1–2 minutes, then add the noodles and stir-fry for a further 2 minutes until heated through. Spoon into a warm serving bowl and serve straight away.

Tip

★ Hoisin sauce is a thick and sticky brownish-red sauce made from soy beans, garlic, chilli, sugar and vinegar. It adds an authentic flavour to many Chinese-style dishes. Once opened, keep it in the fridge – it will last for several months.

beef
lamb
&
pork

Meat is wonderfully flavoursome and can be cooked in a variety of ways to suit every taste and budget. In this chapter you'll find a wide range of meat dishes from beef steaks and lamb chops to minced (ground) meats, sausages and bacon, all ideal for meals in minutes. There are lots of tasty favourites such as Sausage and Mushroom Pie and Navarin of Lamb, as well as more adventurous dishes, including Spicy Tunisian Lamb with Vegetable Couscous.

Beef, lamb and pork provide an excellent concentrated source of protein and many valuable nutrients, particularly the minerals iron and zinc. They can be healthily lean too, with some cuts containing no more fat than chicken. Quick-cooking cuts of meat – perfect for pan-frying, grilling (broiling) and stir-frying – tend to be the tender prime cuts; but though they are more expensive, there's no wastage and a little can go a very long way.

Store meat in the coldest part of the fridge and, if raw, keep it away from cooked foods. Be guided by the 'use by' dates (or freeze in individual portions on the day of purchase); generally, most chops and steaks will keep in the fridge for 2–3 days.

Peppered steak
with potato rosti

Ready in 35 minutes

1 potato, about 100 g/4 oz
15 g/½ oz/1 tbsp unsalted (sweet) butter
a pinch of salt
1.5 ml/¼ tsp mixed peppercorns, crushed
1 medallion steak, about 150 g/5 oz
30 ml/2 tbsp olive oil
15 ml/1 tbsp creamed horseradish
5 ml/1 tsp snipped fresh chives

1 Place the unpeeled potato in a small saucepan, cover with boiling water and simmer for 8 minutes. Remove from the water and leave to cool slightly. Scrape off the skin, then coarsely grate the potato into a bowl. Add the butter and salt and stir until the butter has melted. Shape into two flat rosti cakes.

2 Press the crushed peppercorns into the steak. Heat half the oil in a frying pan, add the steak and fry for 2–3 minutes on each side or until done to your liking. Remove from the pan and keep warm. Wipe out the pan.

3 Heat the remaining oil in the pan, add the potato rostis and fry for 3–4 minutes on each side until golden brown and crisp.

4 Meanwhile, mix together the horseradish and chives. Serve the steak on the rostis, topped with the horseradish and chive sauce.

Serve with: A steamed green vegetable such as broccoli

Tips

★ If time allows, marinate the steak for an hour or two in the fridge in a spoonful of French dressing or a mixture of 15 ml/1 tbsp of olive oil and 5 ml/1 tsp of balsamic condiment (this not only flavours the meat but also helps to tenderise it). Pat the meat dry on kitchen paper (paper towels) before coating with the peppercorns.

★ Try to choose a waxy variety of potato, such as Charlotte, for this dish, as the grated pieces will stick together better.

Cajun-spiced steak
and mushroom fajitas

Ready in 20 minutes

150 g/5 oz rump steak
20 ml/1½ tbsp sunflower oil
2.5 ml/½ tsp Cajun spice mix
½ red onion, sliced
1 large flat mushroom, sliced
salt and freshly ground black pepper
1 soft flour tortilla
15 ml/1 tbsp soured (dairy sour) cream or Greek-style yoghurt
a few sprigs of fresh coriander (cilantro)

1 Trim any fat from the steak. Drizzle with a few drops of the oil, then sprinkle the Cajun spice evenly over. Heat half the oil in a frying pan, add the steak and cook for 4–5 minutes on each side or until done to your liking. Transfer to a warm plate and leave to rest. Wipe out the pan.

2 Heat the remaining oil in the pan, add the onion and stir-fry for 2 minutes. Add the mushroom and cook for 3 more minutes. Season with a little salt and pepper

3 Heat the tortilla in a microwave for 10 seconds, then spread with the soured cream or yoghurt. Cut the steak into thin slices and scatter down the centre of the tortilla. Top with the mushroom and onion mixture and scatter with sprigs of coriander. Roll up tightly and serve straight away.

Serve with: Tortilla chips and a tomato salsa

Tips

★ If time allows, set the seasoned steak aside for 30 minutes to allow the flavours to penetrate.

★ Microwaving the tortilla not only warms it but also makes it more flexible and easy to roll. If you prefer it lightly browned, warm it in a frying pan over a moderate heat for about a minute on each side.

Guinness-marinated
beef steak

Ready in 10 minutes, plus marinating time

For the marinade:
5 ml/1 tsp Dijon mustard
5 ml/1 tsp soft brown sugar
a pinch of ground cloves
75 ml/6 tbsp Guinness or dark ale
For the beef:
1 sirloin or rump steak, about 200 g/7 oz
5 ml/1 tsp olive oil
freshly ground black pepper
chopped fresh flat-leaf parsley to garnish

1 To make the marinade, mix together all the ingredients. Place the steak in a shallow, non-metallic dish, pour the marinade over, cover and place in the fridge for at least 8 hours, turning occasionally if possible.

2 When ready to cook, remove the steak from the marinade and pat dry with kitchen paper (paper towels). Heat a ridged cast-iron grill (broiler) pan or a non-stick frying pan until hot. Rub the steak on both sides with the oil, then season with pepper. Cook the steak for 2½–3½ minutes on each side, depending on how well you like it cooked. Transfer the steak to a warmed plate and allow it to rest for a few minutes.

3 Pour the reserved marinade into the pan and let it bubble for a minute or two until some of the liquid has evaporated and the marinade is thick and syrupy. Drizzle over the steak and serve straight away, sprinkled with chopped parsley.

Serve with: Steamed or boiled new potatoes, baby carrots tossed in a little melted butter and sesame seeds, and a rocket or baby leaf salad

Tips

★ The beer marinade not only flavours the steak but also makes it meltingly tender. If you prefer, red wine can be used instead.

★ It's important to pat the steak 'dry' on kitchen paper before cooking, or it will steam rather than fry and the meat won't brown.

Shish kebabs
with onion salsa

 Ready in 15 minutes

For the salsa:
½ red onion, halved and thinly sliced
5 ml/1 tsp chopped mint leaves
juice of ½ lime
salt and freshly ground black pepper
For the kebabs:
½ small green chilli, seeded and finely chopped, or 2.5 ml/½ tsp chilli paste from a jar
a pinch of ground ginger
1.5 ml/¼ tsp garlic salt or ordinary salt
5 ml/1 tsp sun-dried tomato purée (paste)
15 ml/1 tbsp chopped fresh coriander (cilantro)
5 ml/1 tsp sunflower oil
150 g/5 oz lean minced (ground) beef

1 To make the salsa, combine all the ingredients in a small bowl. Set aside to allow the flavours to mingle.

2 To make the kebabs, place all the ingredients in a bowl and mix well, then divide into three portions. Lightly oil three metal kebab skewers and mould one portion of the meat mixture around each to form a sausage shape.

3 Preheat the grill (broiler) to moderately hot and line the grill pan with foil. Place the kebabs on the grill rack and cook for 3–4 minutes on each side or until well browned and cooked through. Serve hot with the salsa.

Serve with: Warm naan bread and lettuce leaves

Tips

★ You can buy small amounts of minced beef from the butcher or at the supermarket meat counter. If you buy it in larger packs, divide it into smaller meal-sized portions and pack it into freezer bags. Flatten the meat slightly in the bags to make stacking easier and so that it thaws more quickly.

★ Sun-dried tomato purée contains lots of additional seasonings including hot chillies, garlic, oregano and capers, so it gives extra flavour without the need for lots of individual ingredients.

Spicy tunisian lamb
with vegetable couscous

 Ready in 25 minutes

150 g/5 oz lean minced (ground) lamb

10 ml/2 tsp plain yoghurt

5 ml/1 tsp harissa or chilli paste

1 small garlic clove, peeled and crushed, or 2.5 ml/½ tsp garlic purée (paste)

15 ml/1 tbsp chopped fresh coriander (cilantro)

salt and freshly ground black pepper

6 large ready-to-eat dried apricots

For the couscous:

150 ml/¼ pint/⅔ cup hot vegetable stock

25 g/1 oz green beans, trimmed and cut into short lengths

1 small carrot, cut into matchsticks

50 g/2 oz/⅓ cup couscous

a few slices of red onion to garnish (optional)

1 Place the lamb, yoghurt, harissa or chilli paste, garlic and coriander in a bowl. Season with salt and pepper and mix well. Divide the mixture into four portions and form each into a sausage shape. Thread two lamb portions and three apricots alternately on to two metal skewers.

2 To make the couscous, bring the stock to the boil in a small saucepan. Add the beans and carrot and simmer for 3 minutes. Add the couscous to the pan, stir, then turn off the heat. Cover with a lid and leave for 12–15 minutes.

3 Meanwhile, preheat the grill (broiler) to moderately hot and line the grill pan with foil. Place the lamb skewers on the grill rack and cook for 12–15 minutes, turning occasionally, until the lamb is cooked through. Fluff up the couscous with a fork and serve with the lamb skewers, garnished with onion slices, if liked.

Serve with: A crisp green salad

Tip

★ If time allows, soak the apricots in a little orange or apple juice for 20–40 minutes. This not only flavours them but also makes them plump and juicy and less likely to dry out and burn on the skewers.

Navarin of lamb

 Ready in 45 minutes (Makes 2 servings)

10 ml/2 tsp plain (all-purpose) flour
salt and freshly ground black pepper
350 g/12 oz lamb neck fillet, trimmed and diced
20 ml/1½ tbsp olive oil
1 small onion, peeled and chopped
1 carrot, peeled and thickly sliced
1 small parsnip, peeled and thickly sliced
200 g/7 oz/1 small can of chopped tomatoes
5 ml/1 tsp sun-dried tomato purée (paste)
150 ml/¼ pint/⅔ cup red wine
1 bay leaf
1 sprig of fresh parsley
1 sprig of fresh thyme
200 g/7 oz/1 small can of cannellini beans, drained
30 ml/2 tbsp chopped fresh parsley

1 Season the flour with a little salt and pepper and use to lightly coat the pieces of lamb.

2 Heat 15 ml/1 tbsp of the oil in a non-stick saucepan and add the lamb. Fry over a high heat for 2–3 minutes, stirring frequently, until browned all over. Remove with a slotted spoon, leaving any fat behind, and set aside.

3 Add the remaining oil to the pan, add the onion and cook for 5 minutes. Add the carrot and parsnip and cook for a further 2 minutes. Stir in the tomatoes, tomato purée, wine and lamb.

4 Tie together the bay leaf, parsley and thyme sprigs with string and add to the mixture. Cover with a lid and cook over a gentle heat for 25 minutes or until the lamb and vegetables are tender.

5 Stir in the beans and simmer for a further 5 minutes. Remove the herbs, then stir in the chopped parsley and season well with salt and pepper.

6 Spoon half the casserole into a bowl or freezer container and allow to cool. Serve the remainder at once.

Serve with: Creamed potatoes and steamed cabbage

Second serving: Either cover the cooled casserole and chill in the fridge for the following day, or freeze for up to a month. If frozen, allow to thaw in the fridge overnight. To serve, heat gently in a saucepan, allowing it to bubble for a few minutes to ensure it is piping hot.

Nut-crusted
lamb chops

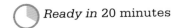 *Ready in* 20 minutes

15 ml/1 tbsp plain (all-purpose) flour
salt and freshly ground black pepper
2 lamb chops, trimmed
1 small egg, lightly beaten
50 g/2 oz/½ cup chopped mixed nuts
15 ml/1 tbsp olive oil
1 small garlic clove, crushed, or 2.5 ml/½ tsp garlic purée (paste)
5 ml/1 tsp chopped fresh rosemary
½ x 200 g/7 oz/small can of flageolet beans, drained and rinsed
½ x 200 g/7 oz/small can of chopped tomatoes
sprigs of fresh rosemary to garnish

1 Preheat the oven to 200°C/400°F/gas 6/fan oven 180°C. Season the flour with a little salt and pepper and use to lightly coat both sides of the lamb. Dip the chops first in the beaten egg, then in the nuts, gently pressing them down. Repeat on the other side of the chops.

2 Heat half the oil in a non-stick frying pan, add the chops and fry for 1½ minutes on each side until browned. Transfer them to a baking tray and cook in the oven for 8–12 minutes or until they are cooked to your liking.

3 Meanwhile, wipe the frying pan clean with kitchen paper (paper towels). Add the remaining oil and the garlic and rosemary and fry for 1 minute. Add the beans and tomatoes, then simmer gently for 5 minutes until slightly thickened.

4 Serve the chops, garnished with sprigs of rosemary, with the bean and tomato mixture.

Serve with: Steamed or boiled new potatoes or a jacket potato

Tips

★ Transfer the remaining half-cans of the beans and tomatoes to small containers, cover and store in the fridge for up to 3 days, or freeze.

★ Cook a jacket potato in the microwave until just tender. Add to the oven at the same time as the chops to make the skin crisp.

Sausage, mash
and mushroom pie

 Ready in 40 minutes

100 g/4 oz ready-rolled puff pastry (paste)
milk for brushing
100 g/4 oz leftover mashed potato
15 g/½ oz/1 tbsp butter
5 ml/1 tsp sunflower oil
½ small onion, thinly sliced
50 g/2 oz button mushrooms, quartered
4 cooked mini sausages or 2 ready-cooked frankfurters, thickly sliced
75 ml/5 tbsp chicken or beef gravy made from gravy granules
salt and freshly ground black pepper
15 ml/1 tbsp chopped fresh parsley
sprigs of fresh parsley to garnish (optional)

1 Preheat the oven to 220°C/425°F/gas 7/fan oven 200°C. Cut the pastry into a rectangle or oval about 18 cm/7 in × 13 cm/5 in. Brush with milk, transfer to a baking (cookie) sheet lined with baking parchment and bake for 15 minutes.

2 Meanwhile, mix the potato with half the butter. Turn down the oven to 160°C/325°F/gas 3/fan oven 145°C, cover the potato with foil and add to the oven with the pastry and bake for 10 more minutes until the potato is warmed through and the pastry is well risen and lightly browned.

3 Meanwhile, heat the remaining butter and the oil in a frying pan. Add the onion and mushrooms and cook over a moderate heat for 10 minutes, stirring often, until soft and beginning to brown. Add the sausages, pour in the gravy and simmer for 3–4 minutes until heated through. Season to taste with salt and pepper.

4 Split the pastry in half horizontally and put the base on a warmed plate. Spoon in the mashed potato, then top with the sausage mixture. Sprinkle with the chopped parsley and garnish with sprigs of parsley, if liked. Set the top in place and serve straight away.

Serve with: Steamed green beans and carrots

Warm bacon and mushroom
salad with Parmesan croûtons

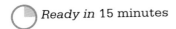 *Ready in* 15 minutes

2 slices of ciabatta, cut into cubes
15 ml/1 tbsp olive oil
15 ml/1 tbsp freshly grated Parmesan cheese
50 g/2 oz smoked bacon pieces
50 g/2 oz button mushrooms, halved
2 spring onions (scallions), thinly sliced
5 cherry tomatoes, halved
10 ml/2 tsp balsamic condiment
50 g/2 oz baby salad leaves

1 Preheat the oven to 190°C/375°F/gas 5/fan oven 170°C. Toss the ciabatta with half the oil and all the Parmesan and place in a single layer on a baking tray. Bake for 8–10 minutes or until lightly browned and crispy.

2 Meanwhile, dry-fry the bacon in a non-stick frying pan for 3–4 minutes until well browned. Remove from the pan with a slotted spoon, leaving any fat behind, and transfer to a plate lined with kitchen paper (paper towels).

3 Add the remaining oil to the pan, add the mushrooms and fry for 2–3 minutes. Add the onions and tomatoes and continue cooking for a further minute until they are beginning to soften. Sprinkle the balsamic condiment over the vegetables in the frying pan and turn off the heat.

4 Put the salad leaves in a serving bowl. Add the hot vegetables and quickly toss together. Scatter with the Parmesan croûtons and bacon and serve.

Tips

★ Make a double batch of croûtons and keep half in an airtight container for sprinkling over salad or soup another day.

★ Instead of Parmesan croûtons, make Parmesan wafers: sprinkle 50 g/ 2 oz of freshly grated Parmesan cheese over baking parchment on a baking tray. Bake at 180°C/350°F/gas 4/fan oven 160°C for 12–15 minutes until the cheese has melted and is crisp and pale golden. Allow to cool, then break into pieces. Scatter over the salad just before serving.

★ If you prefer not to turn on your oven to make this dish, scatter with some bought garlic croûtons instead.

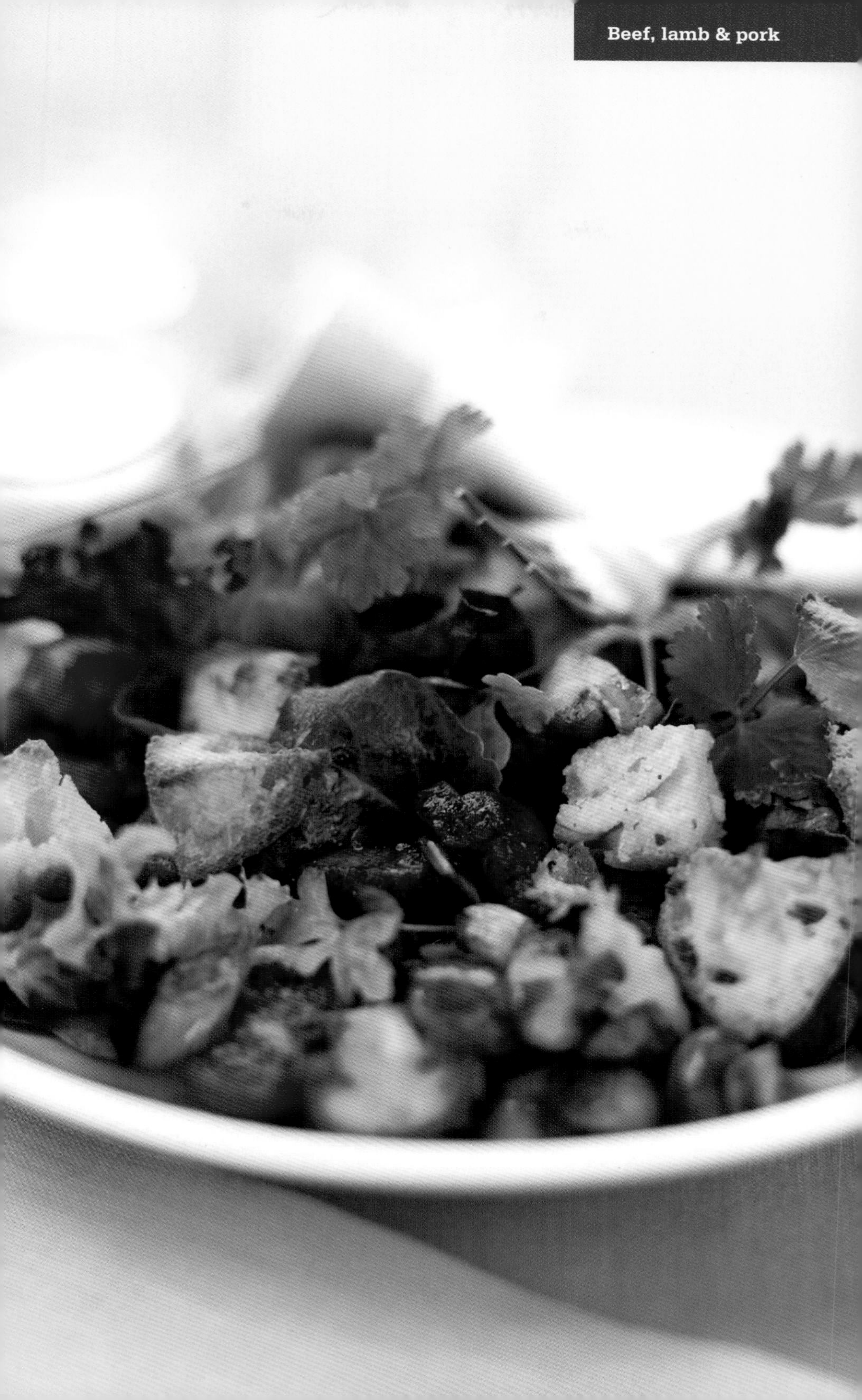

Spicy pork
burgers

Ready in 25 minutes (Makes two servings)

225 g/8 oz minced (ground) pork
5 ml/1 tsp hot curry paste
30 ml/2 tbsp fresh breadcrumbs
½ small red onion, peeled and very finely chopped
juice of ½ lime or 15 ml/1 tbsp bottled lime or lemon juice
½ small red (bell) pepper, seeded and finely chopped
2.5 ml/½ tsp soft light brown sugar
salt and freshly ground black pepper
sunflower oil for shallow frying
fresh mint leaves, to garnish

1 Place all the ingredients in a bowl, seasoning generously with salt and pepper. Using your hands, mix thoroughly.

2 Divide the mixture into six equal portions. Using wet hands, shape each one into a flat, round burger.

3 Heat the oil in a large heavy-based non-stick frying pan over a medium heat, add three of the burgers and fry for 3–4 minutes on each side until well browned and cooked through. Remove and drain on kitchen paper (paper towels). Garnish with mint leaves and serve hot.

Serve with: Boiled or pilau rice, yoghurt and a tomato and cucumber salad or, if you're short of time, with burger buns or chunks of crusty bread and some pre-prepared salad leaves drizzled with French dressing

Tips

★ These burgers freeze really well, so open-freeze the remaining three on a baking tray lined with baking parchment. Once frozen, pack into a freezer-proof container, separating the burgers with baking parchment. Thaw in the fridge overnight and cook as above.

★ Always buy good-quality extra-lean pork mince. It may cost a little more, but is better value as it contains less fat.

★ Lamb or beef mince may be used instead of pork in this recipe.

Ham, egg and cheese
tartlets

Ready in 25 minutes (Makes two servings)

200 g/7 oz ready-rolled puff pastry (paste)
75 g/3 oz/¾ cup grated mature Cheddar cheese
4 thin slices of ham
5 ml/1 tsp Dijon mustard
2 eggs
30 ml/2 tbsp double (heavy) cream
freshly ground black pepper
15 ml/1 tbsp chopped fresh parsley to garnish (optional)

1 Remove the pastry from the fridge and, if time allows, leave it wrapped at room temperature for 15 minutes (this makes it easier to unroll without cracking, but isn't essential). Preheat the oven to 200°C/400°F/gas 6/ fan oven 180°C.

2 Carefully unroll the pastry, then cut it into two squares each about 10 cm/ 4 in. Use to line two large Yorkshire pudding tins, trimming off the edges.

3 Sprinkle 50 g/2 oz of the cheese between the two pastry cases. Top each with 2 slices of ham, thinly spread with mustard, then break an egg over each. Drizzle the cream over, then sprinkle with the remaining cheese and a little pepper.

4 Bake for 15–20 minutes or until the pastry is well risen and golden and the eggs are just cooked. Sprinkle with chopped parsley, if liked, before serving one of the tarts hot.

Serve with: A sliced tomato and basil salad

Second serving: Allow the second tart to cool completely, then put on a plate, cover with clingfilm (plastic wrap) and keep in the fridge for up to 24 hours. Serve chilled or at room temperature.

Tip

★ If the slices of ham are large, trim them to fit and add the trimmings to the tarts as well.

Pork and pepper
koftas

Ready in 25 minutes

100 g/4 oz minced (ground) pork
½ red chilli, seeded and very finely chopped, or a pinch of chilli powder
2 cm/¾ in piece of fresh root ginger, peeled and grated, or 7.5 ml/1½ tsp ginger purée (paste)
1 garlic clove, peeled and finely chopped, or 2.5 ml/½ tsp garlic purée (paste)
10 ml/2 tsp chopped fresh mint
salt and freshly ground black pepper
½ small yellow or red (bell) pepper, seeded and cut into 2.5 cm/1 in pieces
fresh coriander (cilantro) or mint leaves to garnish

1 Put the pork in a bowl and, using your hands, mix in the chilli, ginger, garlic, mint and some salt and pepper. Divide the mixture into six portions.

2 Press the mixture on to two soaked bamboo or lightly oiled metal skewers, alternating with pepper pieces.

3 Preheat the grill (broiler) to moderately hot and line the grill pan with foil. Place the koftas on the grill rack and cook for 8–10 minutes, turning occasionally, until cooked through.

Serve with: Steamed or boiled rice or fingers of warmed pitta bread, Greek-style yoghurt and finely sliced red onion.

Tips

★ If preferred, leave out the fresh chilli and serve the koftas drizzled with chilli sauce.

★ Instead of adding fresh mint to the koftas, serve them with a simple minted yoghurt sauce made by stirring 5 ml/1 tsp of mint sauce into 60 ml/4 tbsp of Greek-style yoghurt.

★ Make double the quantity of the pork mixture and shape the second half into ovals. Open-freeze until solid, then pack into a freezerproof container or bag. Thread on to skewers with pieces of pepper or baby button mushrooms while still half-frozen, then cook when completely thawed.

fish & seafood

Succulent and delicate, the best way to cook fish is fast, making it ideal for super-quick suppers. It's also a very healthy choice as it's a great source of protein and provides many vitamins and minerals. You should eat oily fish such as salmon, tuna or sardines at least once a week as it contains beneficial heart-healthy fats. Try Lime and Ginger Salmon with Fruit Salsa or Griddled Sardines with Lentils and Tomatoes. White fish has very lean flesh and is low in fat, making it an ideal food for helping to maintain a healthy weight.

When buying fish, remember that if it's really fresh it shouldn't smell 'fishy'. Obviously, it's difficult to test pre-packed fish for freshness, but buy from a reliable source and make sure that it looks firm and moist. Both fresh and frozen seafood should be put in the fridge or freezer as soon as possible and, ideally, fresh fish should be eaten on the day you buy it.

Marinated hake
with stir-fried vegetables

 Ready in 25 minutes

1 thick hake fillet, about 175 g/6 oz
zest of ½ small lemon
5 ml/1 tsp chilli oil
15 ml/1 tbsp sesame or sunflower oil
½ x 300 g/10 oz packet of stir-fry vegetables
10 ml/2 tsp dark soy sauce
5 ml/1 tsp clear honey
15 ml/1 tbsp sherry or orange juice
Wedges of lemon to garnish

1 Put the fish in a shallow dish. Mix the lime zest with the chilli oil and rub over the fish. Cover and leave to marinate in a cool place for 10 minutes.

2 Preheat the grill (broiler) to moderate and line the grill pan with foil. Place the fish on the grill rack and cook for 3–4 minutes. Carefully turn over and cook for a further 2–3 minutes or until it is cooked through.

3 Meanwhile, heat the sesame or sunflower oil in a non-stick frying pan. Add the vegetables and stir-fry for 3 minutes. Add the soy sauce, honey and sherry or orange juice. Cook for a further 1–2 minutes or until the vegetables are tender.

4 Spoon the vegetables on to a warm plate and place the fish on top. Serve straight away garnished with wedges of lemon to squeeze over.

Serve with: Boiled 3-minute noodles

Tips

★ Any firm fish fillet may be used for this dish. Try haddock, fresh tuna, salmon or cod for a change – or ask for advice at the fish counter.

★ If you haven't any chilli oil, use extra sesame or sunflower oil instead and add a small pinch of chilli powder or crushed dried chilli flakes.

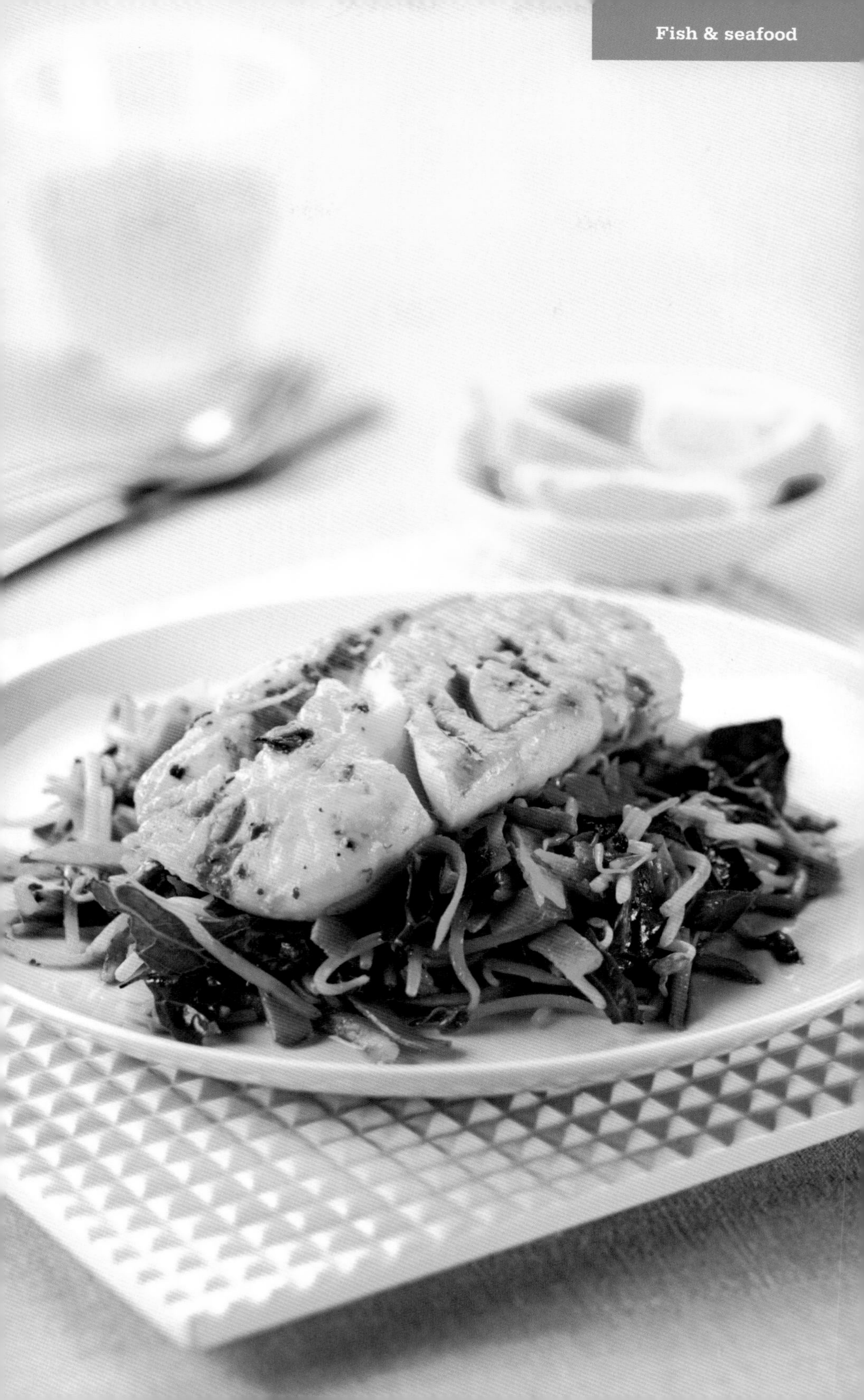

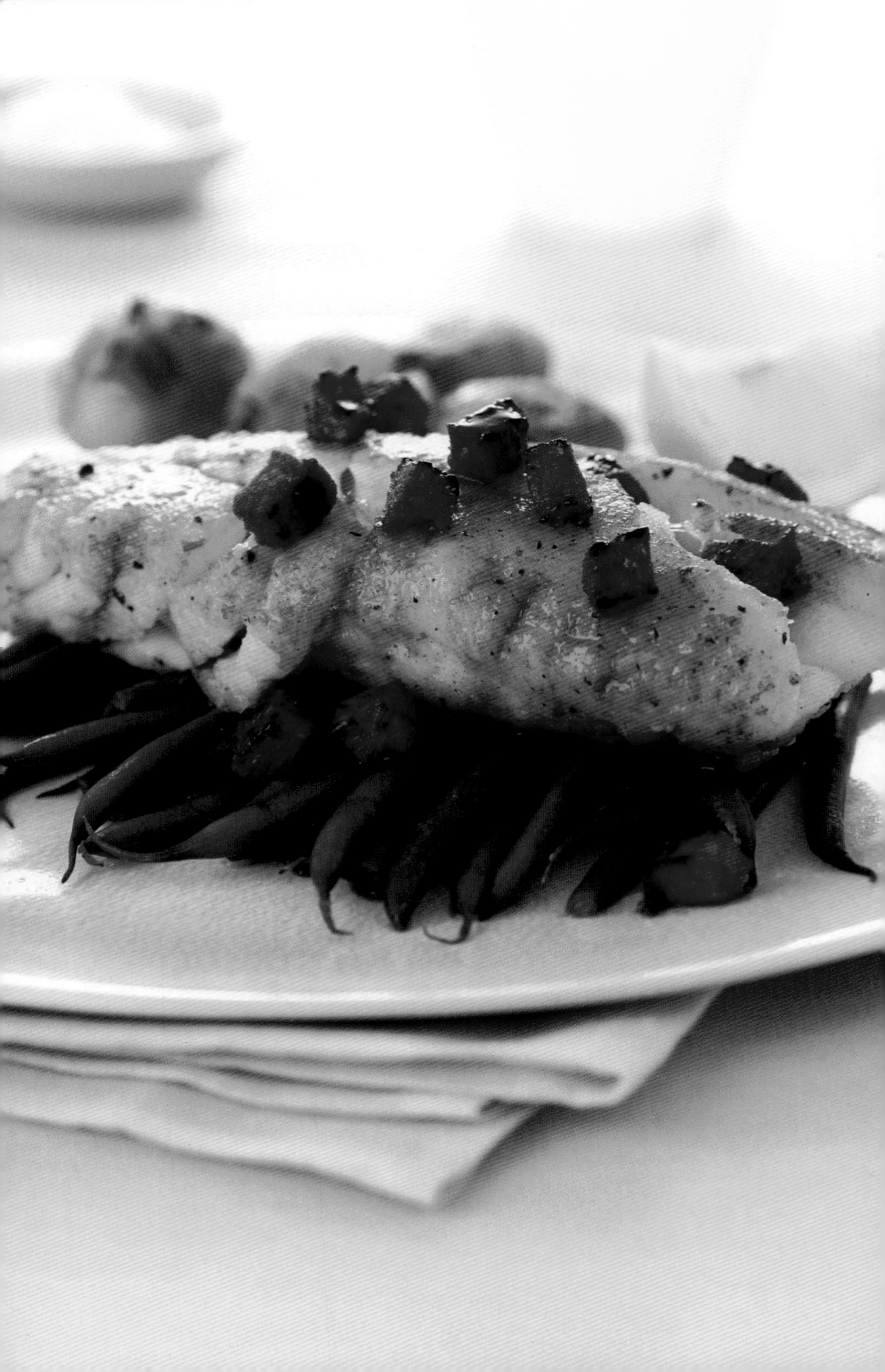

Cod with frizzled chorizo
and crushed new potatoes

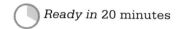 *Ready in* 20 minutes

200 g/7 oz cold cooked or canned new potatoes, drained

15 ml/1 tbsp olive oil

5 ml/1 tsp fresh or bottled lemon juice

30 ml/2 tbsp water

15 ml/1 tbsp chopped fresh parsley

salt and freshly ground black pepper

50 g/2 oz chorizo sausage, diced

15 ml/1 tbsp plain (all-purpose) flour

200 g/7 oz cod loin fillet or other firm white fish, thawed if frozen

1 Lightly crush the potatoes with a wooden spoon, so that a few cracks open up in each. Heat the oil in a non-stick saucepan, add the potatoes and cook for 3 minutes, stirring occasionally, until golden and slightly crispy.

2 Add the lemon juice and water to the potatoes, cover the pan and cook gently for 4 minutes until hot. Remove the lid and continue cooking until the liquid evaporates. Stir in the parsley and season with salt and pepper.

3 Meanwhile, heat a non-stick frying pan over a high heat, add the chorizo and cook for 1–2 minutes until browned and crispy. Remove from the pan with a slotted spoon, leaving the fat behind. Drain on kitchen paper (paper towels). Turn down the heat a little.

4 Season the flour with salt and pepper. Pat the cod dry on kitchen paper, then dust lightly with the flour. Add the cod to the pan and fry over a medium heat for 3–4 minutes on each side or until cooked through. Serve the cod scattered with the chorizo and accompanied by the crushed new potatoes.

Serve with: Steamed or boiled fine green beans

Tip

★ One of the easiest ways to cook one portion of vegetables is in the microwave. Put about 100 g/4 oz of the prepared vegetable in a dish with 45 ml/3 tbsp of water or vegetable stock. Cover with clingfilm (plastic wrap) and make a small hole with a knife to let just a little steam escape. Cook on High for 4–5 minutes, stirring half-way through cooking if possible. Leave to stand for a minute or two to finish cooking, then drain and season before serving.

Spaghetti
vongole

 Ready in 15 minutes (Makes two servings)

15 ml/1 tbsp olive oil

1 large clove garlic, peeled and crushed, or 5 ml/1 tsp garlic purée (paste)

1 red chilli, seeded and finely diced, or 5 ml/1 tsp chilli paste

280 g/10 oz/1 medium can of baby clams (vongole)

100 ml/3½ fl oz/scant ½ cup white wine

250 g/9 oz spaghetti

200 g/7 oz/1 small can of chopped tomatoes

15 ml/1 tbsp chopped fresh parsley

freshly ground black pepper

1 Gently heat the oil, garlic and chilli together in a saucepan for 2–3 minutes without allowing it to colour. Drain the juice from the clams into the pan, add the wine and boil rapidly to reduce until the sauce looks syrupy.

2 Meanwhile, cook the spaghetti in plenty of boiling lightly salted water for 8–10 minutes or according to the packet instructions until *al dente* (tender, but still firm to the bit).

3 Stir the tomatoes and parsley into the sauce and cook for 2 minutes. Add the clams and heat through gently. Drain the spaghetti and toss with the clam sauce, adding pepper to taste. Serve in warm bowls.

Tips

★ Don't add any salt to this dish before you've tasted it; clams often come in a briny liquid.

★ If you don't want to buy a whole bottle of wine just for this dish, look out for 'taster' bottles and small cans of wine. Always choose a wine that you'd also enjoy drinking, as very cheap 'cooking' wines often spoil the flavour of a dish.

★ If you want to make this a very generous and rich serving for one, reduce the spaghetti by about a half.

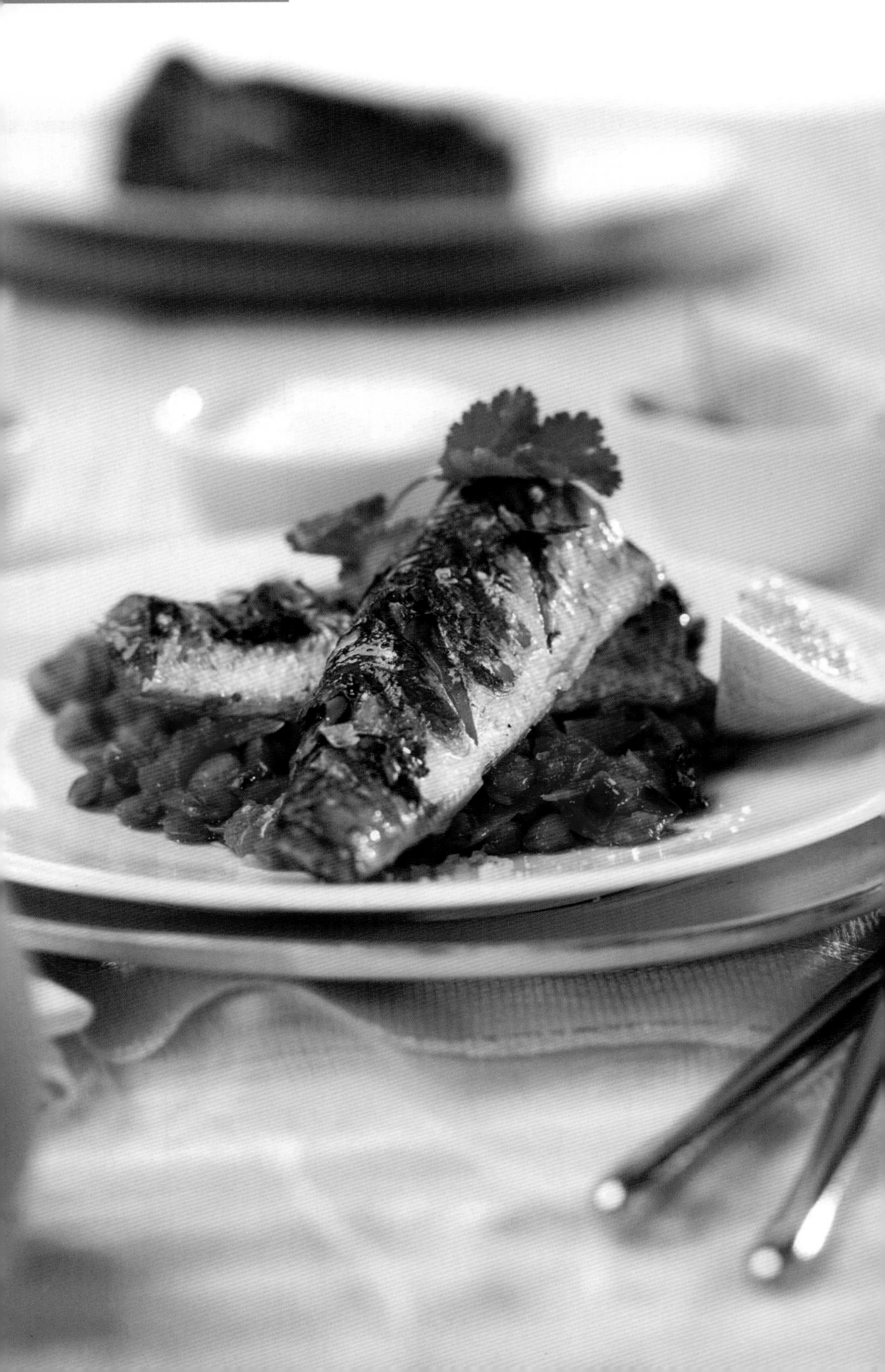

Griddled sardines
with lentils and tomatoes

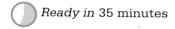 *Ready in* 35 minutes

15 ml/1 tbsp olive oil

½ red onion, peeled and finely chopped

a pinch of dried chilli flakes

200 g/7 oz/1 small can of green lentils, drained and rinsed

2 ripe tomatoes, quartered and chopped

30 ml/2 tbsp water

2 or 3 fresh sardines, cleaned and scaled

15 ml/1 tbsp chopped fresh coriander (cilantro) (optional)

salt and freshly ground black pepper

a sprig of fresh coriander to garnish (optional)

1 Heat the oil in a non-stick frying pan, add the onion and cook for 4–5 minutes until beginning to soften. Add the chilli flakes and cook for a further 2 minutes.

2 Stir in the lentils, tomatoes and water. Bring to a gentle simmer and cook for 2–3 minutes, stirring frequently.

3 Meanwhile, make several shallow diagonal slashes on each side of the sardines. Toss in the chopped coriander, if using, and season generously with salt and pepper.

4 Heat a ridged cast-iron grill (broiler) pan or non-stick frying pan until hot. Add the sardines and cook for 3–4 minutes, then turn over and cook for a further 3–4 minutes, until lightly charred and cooked through. Pile the lentil mixture on to a warm serving plate, top with the sardines and serve straight away, garnished with a sprig of coriander, if liked.

Serve with: Brown crusty rolls and wedges of lemon

Tip

★ If the sardines aren't already prepared, cut off the heads and any fins with kitchen scissors. Wash the insides and outsides under cold running water. If you prefer to cook them under a grill, line the grill pan with foil and place the sardines on a lightly oiled grill rack. Grill (broil) under a moderate heat for 4–5 minutes on each side.

Oriental prawn, pepper
and pineapple noodles

🕐 *Ready in* 20 minutes

75 g/3 oz fine Chinese egg noodles

10 ml/2 tsp sesame or sunflower oil

1 small red or yellow (bell) pepper (or ½ of each), seeded and thinly sliced

5 ml/1 tsp cornflour (cornstarch)

5 ml/1 tsp soft light brown sugar

5 ml/1 tsp red wine vinegar

5 ml/1 tsp sun-dried tomato purée (paste)

60 ml/4 tbsp pineapple juice (from the can)

10 ml/2 tsp dark soy sauce

100 g/4 oz cooked, peeled prawns, preferably tiger prawns, thawed if frozen

75 g/3 oz canned pineapple, cut into bite-sized chunks

15 ml/1 tbsp chopped fresh coriander (cilantro) or parsley

1 Cook the noodles in boiling lightly salted water for 3 minutes or according to the packet instructions. Drain well and set aside.

2 Heat the oil in a wok or non-stick frying pan. Add the pepper slices and stir-fry for 3–4 minutes.

3 Mix the cornflour with the sugar, vinegar, tomato purée, pineapple juice and soy sauce. Add to the pan and cook for a few seconds until thickened, then stir in the prawns and pineapple and cook gently for 1 minute.

4 Add the drained noodles and gently toss everything together over a low heat for about 1 minute until warmed through. Serve straight away, sprinkled with the chopped coriander or parsley.

Tips

★ You could make this stir-fry with strips of shredded cooked chicken instead of prawns.

★ For a crunchy texture, before stir-frying the peppers, dry-fry a small handful of cashew nuts in the wok or frying pan over a medium heat for 2–3 minutes or until golden brown. Remove from the pan and set aside. Scatter over the stir-fry when serving.

★ For extra flavour, boil the noodles in vegetable stock instead of water.

★ For an even faster stir-fry (and to save on washing up), use a 150 g/5 oz pack of straight-to-wok fine or medium noodles instead of dried.

King prawns
with fresh chilli and ginger

Ready in 10 minutes

150 g/5 oz unpeeled cooked king or tiger prawns
15 ml/1 tbsp sunflower oil
5 ml/1 tsp sesame oil or sunflower oil
5 ml/1 tsp grated fresh root ginger or ginger purée (paste)
1 garlic clove, finely sliced
½ small red chilli, seeded and very finely chopped
15 ml/1 tbsp fresh or bottled lemon juice
salt and freshly ground black pepper
15 ml/1 tbsp chopped fresh coriander (cilantro)
wedges of lemon and sprigs of fresh coriander to garnish

1   Remove the heads and peel the prawns but leave the tails on (these make a good 'handle' when eating with the fingers). Briefly rinse the prepared prawns under cold water and pat dry on kitchen paper (paper towels).

2   Heat the oils in a non-stick frying pan over a moderate heat. Add the ginger, garlic and chilli and stir-fry for 1 minute, then add the lemon juice and prawns. Stir-fry for 1–2 minutes more or until the prawns are heated through.

3   Season the prawns with salt and pepper and sprinkle with the chopped coriander. Serve straight away while still hot, garnished with the wedges of lemon and sprigs of coriander.

Serve with: Bread or steamed or boiled plain rice

Tips

★   If you use raw prawns, heat the oil and add the prawns with the ginger, garlic and chilli. Stir-fry for 2–3 minutes or until the prawns have turned completely pink and are cooked through.

★   Take care when preparing chillies and always wash your hands well afterwards as the juices can cause burning irritation, especially if you touch your eyes or lips.

★   If you enjoy spicy food, it's worth investing in a small jar of ready-chopped chillies; once opened, they will keep in the fridge for 2–3 months. About 5 ml/1 tsp is the equivalent of one small chilli.

Chilli fried fish
with coriander potatoes

Ready in 25 minutes

150 g/5 oz baby new potatoes

15 ml/1 tbsp olive oil

10–15 ml/2–3 tsp chilli paste such as sambal olek

1 thick haddock fillet, about 175 g/6 oz

a small knob of butter or sunflower margarine

30 ml/2 tbsp chopped fresh coriander (cilantro)

salt and freshly ground black pepper

1 Scrub the potatoes, if necessary, and place them in a small saucepan. Pour over just enough boiling water to cover and simmer gently for about 15 minutes or until they are cooked through.

2 Meanwhile, heat the oil in a non-stick frying pan. Spread the chilli paste over the haddock fillet. Place the fillet, skin-side down, in the frying pan and cook for 4–5 minutes until the skin is crispy and the fish almost cooked through. Turn over and cook for a further 1–2 minutes.

3 Drain the potatoes and return to the pan. Add the butter or margarine, the coriander and some salt and pepper. Toss to coat the potatoes and serve with the fish.

Serve with: Green salad leaves such as rocket

Tips

★ Sambal olek is an Indonesian curry paste or relish, often made with just chopped red chillies, salt and brown sugar, but sometimes with the addition of other ingredients such as ginger, turmeric, lemon grass and aromatic leaves and herbs. Some are fiercely hot because the chilli seeds have been left in, so check the jar and adjust the quantity you use, if necessary.

★ Canned new potatoes make a great storecupboard standby and can be used instead of new potatoes for this recipe, if preferred.

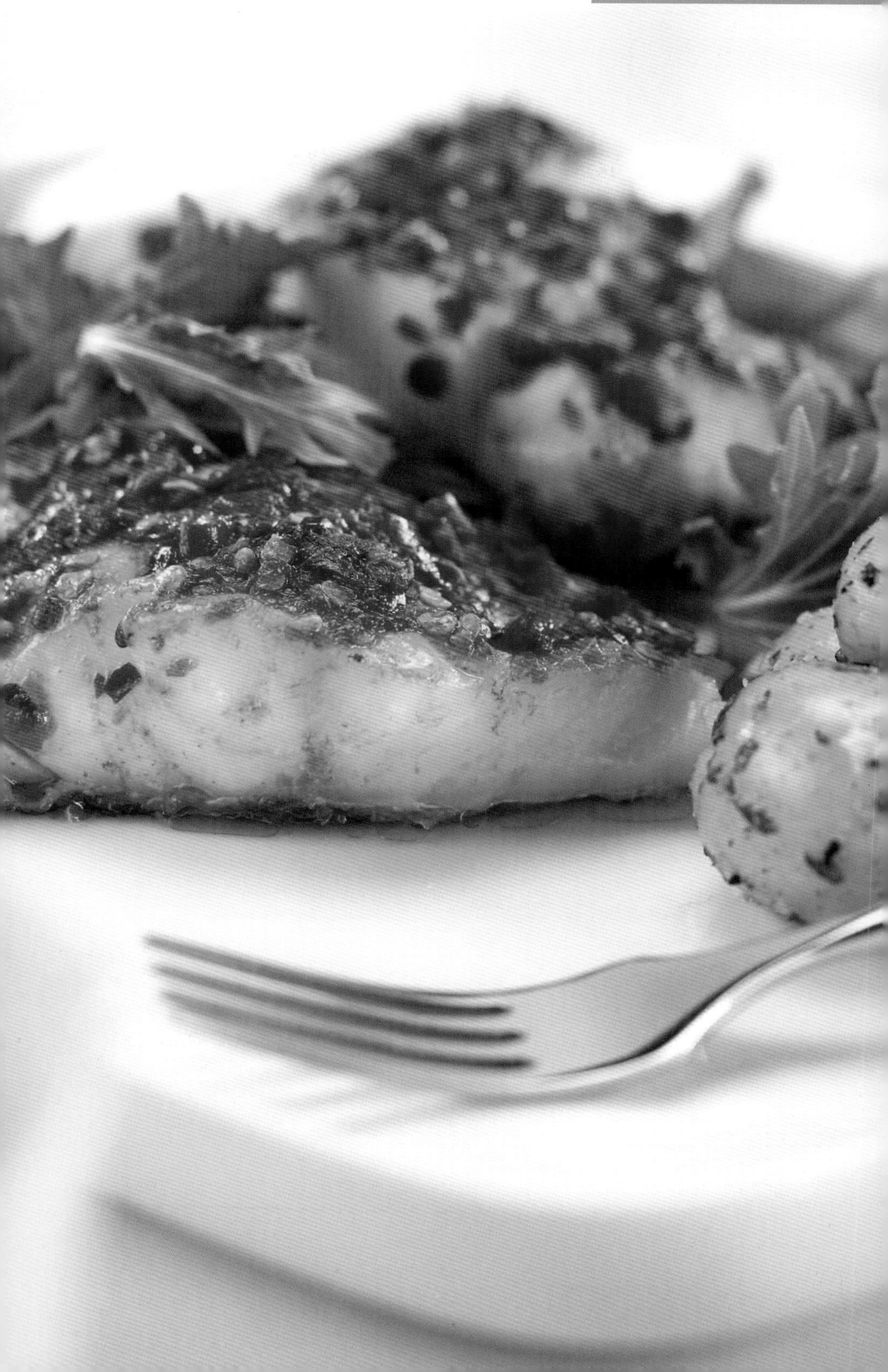

Lemon-dressed fish
with red pepper couscous

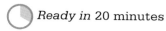 *Ready in* 20 minutes

50 g/2 oz/⅓ cup couscous

100 ml/3½ fl oz/scant ½ cup boiling vegetable stock

150–175 g/5–6 oz thick white fish fillet such as cod or haddock

salt and freshly ground black pepper

15 ml/1 tbsp olive oil

10 ml/2 tsp fresh or bottled lemon juice

½ small red (bell) pepper, seeded and diced

1 tomato, diced

2 spring onions (scallions), trimmed and finely sliced

15 ml/1 tbsp chopped fresh parsley

a large sprig of fresh dill (dill weed) to garnish

1 Put the couscous in a heatproof bowl and pour the stock over. Stir, then cover the bowl with a pan lid to keep in the heat and leave until all the stock has been absorbed and the grains are tender.

2 Meanwhile, cook the fish. Preheat the grill (broiler) to medium and line the grill pan with foil. Season the fish with a little salt and pepper, then place skin-side up on the grill rack. Drizzle with 5 ml/1 tsp of the oil. Cook for 6–7 minutes, without turning, or until the fish is opaque and cooked through.

3 Whisk together the remaining oil and the lemon juice. Stir the diced pepper, tomato, spring onions and parsley into the couscous and season to taste with salt and pepper.

4 Spoon the warm couscous on to a plate and top with the fish. Drizzle the lemon dressing over the top and serve garnished with a sprig of dill.

Serve with: Slices of ciabatta (the sun-dried tomato and olive variety goes especially well)

Tip

★ Make double this quantity of the couscous and serve cold the following day as a salad topped with crumbled Feta cheese or with some sliced cold meat.

Lime and ginger salmon
with fruit salsa

 Ready in 25 minutes

175 g/6 oz salmon fillet, skinned
finely grated zest and juice of ½ lime
1 piece of stem ginger, finely chopped
15 ml/1 tbsp stem ginger syrup
salt and freshly ground black pepper
For the fruit salsa:
50 g/2 oz fresh strawberries, hulled
1 ripe plum, stoned (pitted)
¼ small mango, peeled

1 Preheat the oven to 180°C/350°F/gas 4/fan oven 160°C. Cut out a 30 cm/12 in square of foil or baking parchment and place the salmon steak in the middle. Sprinkle half the lime zest and juice over, then scatter the ginger over and drizzle with the ginger syrup. Season lightly with salt and pepper.

2 Fold over the foil or paper to form a parcel, leaving a little air inside so that the fish can steam, and twist the edges to seal. Place the parcel on a baking tray. Bake for 15 minutes or until the fish is just cooked through.

3 Meanwhile, to make the fruit salsa, chop the strawberries, plum and mango into similar-sized small pieces. Mix with the remaining lime zest and juice and set aside.

4 Carefully open the foil parcel (the steam will be very hot) and transfer the salmon to a warm plate. Serve with the fruit salsa.

Serve with: Steamed or boiled rice or canned new potatoes (put them in an ovenproof dish with a knob of butter, cover tightly with foil and warm in the oven at the same time as the salmon).

Tip

★ Instead of serving with a fruit salsa, cook the salmon on a bed of vegetables: finely shred 75 g/3 oz of mixed Asian greens such as pak choy and Chinese cabbage and arrange in the middle of the foil or paper square. Top with the salmon, then sprinkle with the grated zest and juice of ½ small orange. Fold up and bake as before.

vegetables
&
vegetarian

You don't have to be a vegetarian to enjoy the occasional meat- or fish-free meal, as these delicious dishes show. Eggs make the ultimate impromptu meal for one; not only are they excellent prepared quite simply, such as by boiling or poaching, but they can also be used for easy creative meals such as Egg-fried Rice or Fluffy Baked Egg. They can usually be kept for up to three weeks (check the 'use by' date), so make great fridge fodder. Cheese is also a versatile ingredient, but don't just buy Cheddar; cheeses such as Feta and Mozzarella make a delicious change and have a long fridge life.

If you don't eat meat, there are lots of other protein sources such as nuts and pulses. But do make sure that you get plenty of vitamins and minerals in your diet, including iron – as well as eggs, other non-meat sources of this vital mineral include dried fruit such as apricots and fortified breakfast cereals.

Enjoy the vegetable and vegetarian dishes in this chapter – they are full of flavour and allow you to take full advantage of the wide choice of vegetables in the shops and from many different cuisines.

Feta and pine nut
stuffed pepper

Ready in 25 minutes

1 red or yellow (bell) pepper
15 ml/1 tbsp olive oil
25 g/1 oz/¼ cup pine nuts
1 small garlic clove, peeled and crushed, or 2.5 ml/½ tsp garlic purée (paste)
25 g/1 oz/2 tbsp long-grain rice
100 ml/3½ fl oz/scant ½ cup hot vegetable stock
4 cherry tomatoes, halved
50 g/2 oz Feta or other crumbly cheese, diced or crumbled
15 ml/1 tbsp chopped fresh parsley
salt and freshly ground black pepper

1 Preheat the oven to 200°C/400°F/gas 6/fan oven 180°C. Halve the pepper lengthways and remove the cores and seeds with a sharp knife. Brush the inside with 5 ml/1 tsp of the oil, then place them, cut-sides up, on a small baking tray or ovenproof dish. Bake in the oven for 10 minutes.

2 Heat the remaining oil in a small saucepan. Add the pine nuts and fry gently until pale golden, then remove with a slotted spoon and set aside.

3 Add the garlic to the pan and cook, stirring, for a few seconds. Add the rice and stir to coat in the oil, then pour in the stock. Turn up the heat and quickly bring to the boil. Stir, turn down the heat a little and cover with a lid. Cook the rice for 10 minutes, or according to the packet instructions, or until just tender but still with a little bite (it will cook a little more in the oven). Most of the stock should have been absorbed at this stage.

4 Stir the tomatoes, Feta, parsley and pine nuts into the rice mixture. Season to taste with salt and pepper.

5 Spoon the stuffing mixture into the pepper halves. Add 45 ml/3 tbsp of warm water to the tray or dish and loosely cover the peppers with foil. Roast for 10 minutes, then remove the foil and roast for a further 5–10 minutes or until the filling is lightly browned and the pepper tender.

Serve with: A mixed baby leaf salad

Tip

★ Flaked (sliced) almonds make a good alternative to pine nuts.

Egg-fried rice

 Ready in 10 minutes

10 ml/2 tsp sunflower oil

½ red or green (bell) pepper, seeded and chopped

2 spring onions (scallions), trimmed and thinly sliced diagonally

15 ml/1 tbsp frozen sweetcorn, thawed

15 ml/1 tbsp frozen peas, thawed

1 egg, lightly beaten

250 g/9 oz/2¼ cups cooked rice

10 ml/2 tsp dark soy sauce

freshly ground black pepper

sliced red and green chillies to garnish (optional)

1 Heat the oil in a small wok or non-stick frying pan over a medium heat. Add the chopped pepper and spring onions and stir-fry for 2 minutes to soften.

2 Add the sweetcorn and peas, then stir in the beaten egg. Leave to cook for 30 seconds, then stir to break up the egg.

3 Add the rice, soy sauce and a little pepper and stir-fry until heated through. Serve in a warm bowl and garnish with chilli slices, if liked.

Serve with: Extra soy sauce, if liked

Tips

★ Leftover rice is perfect for this dish (remember to cook extra the night before). It should be cooled quickly and stored in a covered bowl in the fridge. Always use within 24 hours of cooking and reheat thoroughly.

★ When defrosting vegetables such as peas and sweetcorn, spread them out on a piece of kitchen paper (paper towel) to absorb the moisture. To speed up thawing, put them in a sieve (strainer) and rinse briefly with near-boiling water.

★ Dark soy sauce is richer and less salty than light, though you could use either for this recipe. When a recipe contains soy sauce, always taste before seasoning.

★ Increase the protein in this dish by adding 50 g/2 oz of diced firm tofu (the sesame seed variety works particularly well in this recipe). Lightly fry it in 10 ml/2 tsp of oil before you start cooking the vegetables, then stir it in at the end of cooking.

Spinach and cheese
muffin pizzas

 Ready in 20 minutes

50 g/2 oz baby spinach leaves
1 wholemeal or white muffin
30 ml/2 tbsp soured (dairy sour) cream or Greek-style yoghurt
2 ripe tomatoes, roughly chopped
salt and freshly ground black pepper
50 g/2 oz Mozzarella cheese, diced
1 spring onion (scallion), trimmed and sliced
5 ml/1 tsp fresh thyme leaves (optional)

1 Put the spinach in a heatproof bowl, cover with clingfilm (plastic wrap) and cook in the microwave for 1½ minutes on High. Alternatively, cook in a covered pan on the hob for 2–3 minutes until wilted. Drain well and squeeze out any excess moisture.

2 Preheat the grill (broiler) to moderately hot. Split the muffin in half and toast lightly on both sides under the grill. Spread the cut side of each half with a little soured cream or yoghurt, then pile on the spinach and tomatoes, seasoning well with salt and pepper.

3 Scatter the Mozzarella over the top, then pop the muffins back under the grill for 2–3 minutes or until the cheese is melting and starting to turn golden brown. Sprinkle the spring onion and thyme leaves, if using, over the muffin pizzas and serve straight away.

Tips

★ Buy a bag of baby spinach leaves and use the rest to make a side salad for another meal – it's delicious with a balsamic dressing made by whisking 15 ml/1 tbsp of olive oil with 10 ml/2 tsp of balsamic condiment and a tiny amount of Dijon mustard.

★ Spring onions are a great buy when you're cooking for one, as ordinary onions are often too large when preparing small quantities of food. Keep them in a paper or an open plastic bag (to allow air to circulate) in the salad drawer in the fridge.

★ If you like skinned tomatoes, put them in a bowl and cover with boiling water. Leave to stand for about 45 seconds, then drain and rinse under cold water; the skins will slip off easily.

Fluffy baked egg
with pepper and spinach

🕐 *Ready in* 30 minutes

75 g/3 oz/¾ cup penne pasta

5 ml/1 tsp olive oil

1 small garlic clove, peeled and chopped

½ small red (bell) pepper, seeded and sliced

75 g/3 oz baby spinach leaves

15 ml/1 tbsp Mascarpone cheese

15 ml/1 tbsp grated Parmesan cheese

a pinch of freshly grated nutmeg

salt and freshly ground black pepper

1 egg, separated

1 Preheat the oven to 190°C/375°F/gas 5/fan oven 170°C. Cook the pasta in boiling lightly salted water for 8–10 minutes, or according to the packet instructions, until *al dente* (tender, but still firm to the bite).

2 Meanwhile, heat the oil in a frying pan, add the garlic and sliced pepper and cook for 3–4 minutes. Add the spinach and cook, stirring frequently, for 1–2 minutes until it has wilted. Stir in the Mascarpone, half the Parmesan and the nutmeg. Season with salt and pepper.

3 Drain the pasta and stir it into the spinach mixture. Spoon into a lightly buttered individual serving dish and make a large hollow in the centre. Whisk the egg white until stiff, then spoon into the hollow and top with the egg yolk. Bake in the oven for 3–4 minutes, then serve sprinkled with the rest of the Parmesan and a little ground black pepper.

Serve with: Warmed baguette slices

Tips

★ If you don't want to put on the oven just for this dish, you can grill (broil) it instead. Prepare as before using a flameproof serving dish. Cook under the grill (broiler) for 3–4 minutes, depending on how well you like your egg cooked.

★ Look out for 'quick cook' pasta, which takes only 3–5 minutes to cook. It's an ideal storecupboard standby for those days when you're in a hurry to eat.

Feta and pepper tarts

 Ready in 45 minutes (Makes four servings)

300 g/11 oz ready-to roll shortcrust pastry (basic pie crust)
2 eggs, lightly beaten
50 ml/2 fl oz double (heavy) cream
50 ml/2 fl oz passata (sieved tomatoes)
2.5 ml/½ tsp dried mixed herbs
salt and freshly ground black pepper
100 g/4 oz roasted (bell) peppers, drained
100 g/4 oz Feta cheese, crumbled

1 Take the pastry (paste) out of the fridge and, if time allows, leave it wrapped at room temperature for 15 minutes (this makes it easier to roll without cracking, but isn't essential). Roll out the pastry on a lightly floured surface and use to line four 12 cm/4½ in individual fluted tartlet tins. Prick the bases several times with a fork, then line with baking parchment or foil and fill with ceramic baking beans. Chill for 15 minutes.

2 Put a baking (cookie) sheet in the oven and preheat to 200°C/400°F/gas 6/ fan oven 180°C. Place the pastry cases on the baking sheet and bake blind for 8 minutes. Remove the baking parchment and beans and bake for another 5 minutes or until the pastry is coming away from the edges of the tins.

3 Meanwhile, mix together the eggs, cream, passata and herbs. Season with salt and pepper. Divide the peppers between the cases, then spoon the egg mixture over. Scatter the Feta over, then return the tarts to the oven and bake for 15 minutes or until lightly set. Remove from the tins and serve warm.

Serve with: Lightly fried courgette slices or ribbons (cut these from a trimmed courgette using a vegetable peeler)

Tips

★ You can buy roasted peppers from the deli counter or in jars in flavoured oil. Drain well before using, keeping the oil. They can be used in cooking and salad dressings.

★ To freeze the remaining tarts, allow them to cool on a wire rack, then open-freeze on a baking sheet until solid. Wrap each individually in foil and return them to the freezer for up to 1 month. To reheat, thaw at room temperature, still wrapped, for 30 minutes (or overnight in the fridge), then reheat in a preheated oven at 180°C/350°F/gas 4/fan oven 160°C for 10–15 minutes. Alternatively, the tarts may be served cold.

Pasta and vegetable
ribbons

 Ready in 15 minutes

75 g/3 oz dried tagliatelle or pappardelle pasta

1 carrot, peeled

1 small courgette (zucchini), trimmed

50 g/2 oz tiny broccoli florets

15 ml/1 tbsp olive oil

15 ml/1 tbsp chopped fresh parsley

salt and freshly ground black pepper

grated Parmesan cheese to serve

1 Cook the pasta in plenty of boiling lightly salted water for 8–10 minutes, or according to the packet instructions, until *al dente* (tender, but still firm to the bite).

2 Meanwhile, use a vegetable peeler to slice the carrot and courgette into long, thin ribbons. Add the broccoli to the pasta for the last 3 minutes' cooking time and the carrot and courgette ribbons for the last 1 minute.

3 Drain the pasta and vegetables and toss together with the olive oil and parsley. Season to taste with salt and pepper and serve straight away, sprinkled with Parmesan.

Tips

★ When cooking pasta, always use plenty of boiling water – it should come about half-way up the pan. Bring the water to a rapid boil, pour in the pasta, give it a stir, then quickly bring back to the boil. Turn down the heat just a little so that the water is still boiling, but not too fiercely. You can half-cover the pan with a lid, but don't cover completely or it will boil over.

★ For extra flavour, boil the pasta in vegetable stock instead of just salted water.

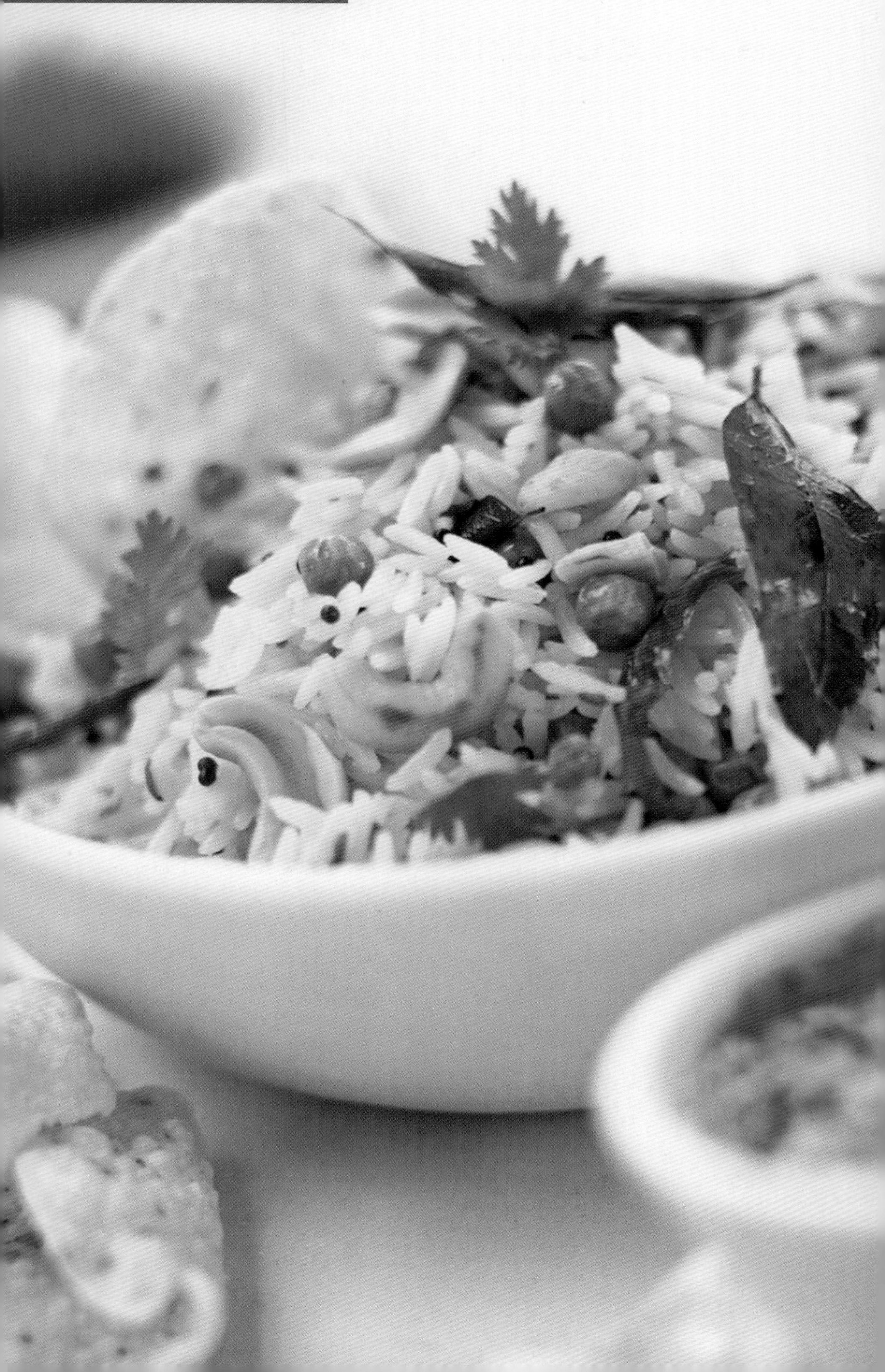

Spiced coconut rice
with cashew nuts

 Ready in 20 minutes (Makes two servings)

100 g/4 oz/½ cup basmati rice
50 g/2 oz creamed coconut
200 ml/7 fl oz/scant 1 cup hot vegetable stock
15 ml/1 tbsp sunflower oil
50 g/2 oz cashew nuts
5 ml/1 tsp cumin seeds
2 curry or bay leaves
1 dried red chilli, cut into thin pieces
50 g/2 oz frozen peas
salt and freshly ground black pepper
fresh coriander (cilantro) leaves to garnish (optional)

1 Rinse the rice in cold water, then drain in a sieve (strainer). Put the creamed coconut in a jug and pour the hot stock over. Stir until dissolved.

2 Heat the oil in a heavy-based non-stick saucepan. Add the cashews and cook over a low heat for 2–3 minutes or until golden. Remove from the pan with a slotted spoon and set aside.

3 Add the cumin seeds, curry or bay leaves and chilli to the pan. Stir-fry for 30 seconds, then add the rice. Cook, stirring, for a few seconds, then add the peas and coconut and stock mixture. Season with salt and pepper.

4 Bring to the boil, stir, then cover the pan tightly. Cook over a very low heat for 10–12 minutes or until the rice is tender and the stock has been absorbed. Do not open the lid for the first 10 minutes or the steam will escape. Fluff up the grains of rice with a fork and serve half in a warm bowl with half the cashew nuts scattered over. Garnish with coriander leaves, if liked.

Serve with: Mini popadoms or warmed naan bread

Tip

★ Creamed coconut is sold in blocks and is a useful ingredient as it can be chopped and mixed with hot stock or water to make the required amount of coconut milk. It will keep for several months in the fridge.

Pasta puttanesca

 Ready in 12 minutes (Makes two servings of sauce)

75 g/3 oz dried penne
For the sauce:
6 ripe plum tomatoes, quartered
1 garlic clove, peeled and chopped
30 ml/2 tbsp olive oil
a handful of fresh flat-leaf parsley, larger stems removed
15 ml/1 tbsp capers, drained
15 ml/1 tbsp black olives
freshly ground black pepper

1 Cook the pasta in boiling water for 8–10 minutes, or according to the packet instructions, until *al dente* (tender, but still firm to the bite).

2 Meanwhile, to make the sauce, put the tomatoes, garlic, oil and parsley in a food processor and blend to a rough purée. Transfer the purée to a saucepan and heat gently until the mixture bubbles. Simmer for 2 minutes, stirring occasionally.

3 Stir in the capers and olives and season the sauce with pepper. Drain the pasta and return it to the pan.

4 Spoon half the sauce over the pasta, then toss together until the pasta is well coated in the sauce and all the ingredients are mixed. Spoon into a warm bowl and serve straight away.

Serve with: A mixed green salad

Second serving: Spoon the rest of the sauce into a bowl and leave to cool, then cover and keep in the fridge for 2–3 days. Gently reheat in a saucepan until bubbling. Try serving it with a different-shaped pasta and perhaps sprinkled with some toasted pine nuts or flaked (sliced) almonds and grated cheese such as Parmesan.

Tip

★ You probably won't need to season this dish with salt as the olives and capers will have plenty already.

Filo-topped
vegetable pie

Ready in 30 minutes

15 ml/1 tbsp cornflour (cornstarch)

100 ml/3½ fl oz/scant ½ cup milk

1.5 ml/¼ tsp dried mixed herbs

¼ vegetable stock cube

40 g/1½ oz/⅓ cup grated Cheddar cheese

225 g/8 oz mixed frozen vegetables such as cauliflower, carrots and peas, thawed

salt and freshly ground black pepper

1 sheet of filo pastry (paste)

10 ml/2 tsp sunflower oil

1 Preheat the oven to 200°C/400°F/gas 6/fan oven 180°C. Mix the cornflour with 30 ml/2 tbsp of the milk in a small saucepan. Stir in the rest of the milk and the herbs and crumble in the stock cube. Bring to the boil, stirring all the time, until the sauce has thickened.

2 Stir the cheese into the sauce, then add the vegetables and season with salt and pepper. Stir well, then spoon the mixture into a small ovenproof dish.

3 Roughly cut the filo pastry into four rectangles. Brush each with a little of the oil, then scrunch up slightly and put on top of the vegetable pie. Bake the pie for 15–20 minutes or until the pastry is golden and crispy.

Serve with: Garlic bread (see below) or a jacket potato (microwave first, then complete cooking in the oven alongside the pie)

Tips

★ Make sure the vegetable mixture is at least 2 cm/¾ in below the rim of the dish or the sauce may bubble over as it cooks in the oven.

★ To make garlic bread, mix 15 g/½ oz/1 tbsp of butter or sunflower margarine with 1 crushed garlic clove or 5 ml/1 tsp of garlic purée (paste), salt and freshly ground black pepper. Using a serrated knife, make several cuts along a baguette roll, about 2.5 cm/1 in apart, as if you were slicing it but not right through (the roll should stay joined at the base). Spread both sides of each slice with garlic butter. Wrap in foil and cook in a preheated oven at 200°C/400°F/gas 6/fan oven 180°C for about 15 minutes.

Index

Page numbers in **bold** refer to illustrations.